Math Expressions

Volume 1

Developed by
The Children's Math Worlds Research Project

PROJECT DIRECTOR AND AUTHOR
Dr. Karen C. Fuson

This material is based upon work supported by the
National Science Foundation
under Grant Numbers
ESI-9816320, REC-9806020, and RED-935373.

Any opinions, findings, and conclusions, or recommendations expressed in this material
are those of the author and do not necessarily reflect the views of the National Science Foundation.

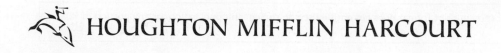

HOUGHTON MIFFLIN HARCOURT

Teacher Reviewers

Kindergarten
Patricia Stroh Sugiyama
Wilmette, Illinois

Barbara Wahle
Evanston, Illinois

Grade 1
Sandra Budson
Newton, Massachusetts

Janet Pecci
Chicago, Illinois

Megan Rees
Chicago, Illinois

Grade 2
Molly Dunn
Danvers, Massachusetts

Agnes Lesnick
Hillside, Illinois

Rita Soto
Chicago, Illinois

Grade 3
Jane Curran
Honesdale, Pennsylvania

Sandra Tucker
Chicago, Illinois

Grade 4
Sara Stoneberg Llibre
Chicago, Illinois

Sheri Roedel
Chicago, Illinois

Grade 5
Todd Atler
Chicago, Illinois

Leah Barry
Norfolk, Massachusetts

Special Thanks

Special thanks to the many teachers, students, parents, principals, writers, researchers, and work-study students who participated in the Children's Math Worlds Research Project over the years.

Credits

Cover art: (t) © Superstock/Alamy, (b) © Steve Bloom Images/Alamy
Illustrative art: Dave Klug
Technical art: Morgan-Cain & Associates

VOLUME 1 CONTENTS

Unit 1 Solve Multiplication and Division Word Problems

1 Class Activity

Show your answers on your paper or in your Activity Workbook.

▶ Checkup for Basic Addition

1. 3 + 9 = ☐   14. 8 + 7 = ☐   27. 8 + 5 = ☐   40. 0 + 8 = ☐

2. 5 + 7 = ☐   15. 6 + 6 = ☐   28. 9 + 8 = ☐   41. 4 + 9 = ☐

3. 8 + 8 = ☐   16. 10 + 9 = ☐   29. 9 + 6 = ☐   42. 6 + 7 = ☐

4. 9 + 5 = ☐   17. 8 + 4 = ☐   30. 7 + 4 = ☐   43. 8 + 9 = ☐

5. 6 + 8 = ☐   18. 0 + 9 = ☐   31. 7 + 6 = ☐   44. 8 + 3 = ☐

6. 9 + 7 = ☐   19. 9 + 4 = ☐   32. 5 + 6 = ☐   45. 8 + 10 = ☐

7. 6 + 4 = ☐   20. 7 + 8 = ☐   33. 7 + 0 = ☐   46. 3 + 2 = ☐

8. 4 + 8 = ☐   21. 5 + 5 = ☐   34. 10 + 10 = ☐   47. 4 + 7 = ☐

9. 3 + 7 = ☐   22. 7 + 9 = ☐   35. 5 + 9 = ☐   48. 6 + 9 = ☐

10. 3 + 8 = ☐   23. 7 + 3 = ☐   36. 7 + 5 = ☐   49. 2 + 3 = ☐

11. 6 + 0 = ☐   24. 3 + 6 = ☐   37. 8 + 6 = ☐   50. 4 + 6 = ☐

12. 7 + 7 = ☐   25. 6 + 5 = ☐   38. 6 + 3 = ☐   51. 9 + 3 = ☐

13. 9 + 9 = ☐   26. 9 + 2 = ☐   39. 4 + 4 = ☐   52. 5 + 8 = ☐

1
Class Activity

Show your answers on your paper or in your Activity Workbook.

▶ Checkup for Basic Subtraction

1. $13 - 8 =$	14. $9 - 9 =$	27. $11 - 9 =$	40. $16 - 9 =$
2. $17 - 9 =$	15. $7 - 4 =$	28. $4 - 0 =$	41. $3 - 0 =$
3. $14 - 5 =$	16. $10 - 8 =$	29. $13 - 7 =$	42. $11 - 5 =$
4. $12 - 3 =$	17. $15 - 9 =$	30. $8 - 2 =$	43. $7 - 7 =$
5. $12 - 9 =$	18. $10 - 6 =$	31. $12 - 4 =$	44. $15 - 7 =$
6. $11 - 7 =$	19. $12 - 5 =$	32. $13 - 6 =$	45. $16 - 7 =$
7. $15 - 8 =$	20. $15 - 6 =$	33. $12 - 6 =$	46. $13 - 5 =$
8. $6 - 6 =$	21. $16 - 8 =$	34. $5 - 5 =$	47. $11 - 4 =$
9. $7 - 0 =$	22. $11 - 8 =$	35. $11 - 6 =$	48. $8 - 0 =$
10. $5 - 2 =$	23. $17 - 8 =$	36. $10 - 4 =$	49. $11 - 3 =$
11. $10 - 9 =$	24. $14 - 7 =$	37. $14 - 9 =$	50. $12 - 8 =$
12. $13 - 9 =$	25. $10 - 7 =$	38. $14 - 6 =$	51. $8 - 6 =$
13. $14 - 8 =$	26. $10 - 5 =$	39. $12 - 7 =$	52. $13 - 4 =$

Subtraction Checkup

▶ Discuss Addition

Vocabulary

Associative Property of Addition

Share and explain methods you could use to solve these addition problems.

1. 9 + 6   **2.** 90 + 60   **3.** 6 + 7   **4.** 60 + 70   **5.** 38 + 6   **6.** 38 + 56

7. Tell word problems for exercises 1, 2, and 6.

▶ Discuss Subtraction

Share and explain methods you could use to solve these subtraction problems.

8. 15 − 9   **9.** 150 − 90   **10.** 13 − 6   **11.** 130 − 60   **12.** 44 − 38   **13.** 94 − 38

14. Tell word problems for exercises 8 and 9.

▶ Add More Than Two Addends

The **Associative Property of Addition** states that grouping the addends in different ways does not change the sum.

90 + 10 + 50

add 90 + 10 first	add 10 + 50 first
(90 + 10) + 50	90 + (10 + 50)
100 + 50	90 + 60
150 = 150	

Parentheses show you which addends to add first.

15. Use the Associative Property of Addition to show a fast way to find 90 + 40.

16. **On the Back** Does the Associative Property work for any numbers? Discuss why or why not.

FLUENCY PLAN LESSON 1

Addition and Subtraction Methods **3**

Class Activity

Show your answers on your paper or in your Activity Workbook.

▶ Checkup for Basic Multiplication

1. $4 \times 5 =$ ▨
2. $1 \times 10 =$ ▨
3. $3 \times 5 =$ ▨
4. $8 \times 5 =$ ▨
5. $4 \times 10 =$ ▨
6. $9 \times 5 =$ ▨
7. $8 \times 2 =$ ▨
8. $6 \times 5 =$ ▨
9. $5 \times 10 =$ ▨
10. $9 \times 2 =$ ▨
11. $5 \times 5 =$ ▨
12. $8 \times 10 =$ ▨
13. $7 \times 2 =$ ▨
14. $5 \times 2 =$ ▨
15. $6 \times 10 =$ ▨
16. $0 \times 5 =$ ▨
17. $6 \times 2 =$ ▨
18. $7 \times 5 =$ ▨

19. $4 \times 3 =$ ▨
20. $9 \times 1 =$ ▨
21. $7 \times 3 =$ ▨
22. $8 \times 0 =$ ▨
23. $5 \times 3 =$ ▨
24. $6 \times 1 =$ ▨
25. $5 \times 0 =$ ▨
26. $9 \times 3 =$ ▨
27. $5 \times 1 =$ ▨
28. $8 \times 3 =$ ▨
29. $6 \times 0 =$ ▨
30. $6 \times 3 =$ ▨
31. $9 \times 0 =$ ▨
32. $1 \times 3 =$ ▨
33. $4 \times 1 =$ ▨
34. $3 \times 3 =$ ▨
35. $3 \times 0 =$ ▨
36. $2 \times 3 =$ ▨

37. $6 \times 4 =$ ▨
38. $9 \times 9 =$ ▨
39. $5 \times 9 =$ ▨
40. $8 \times 4 =$ ▨
41. $6 \times 9 =$ ▨
42. $7 \times 4 =$ ▨
43. $4 \times 9 =$ ▨
44. $9 \times 4 =$ ▨
45. $10 \times 9 =$ ▨
46. $5 \times 4 =$ ▨
47. $7 \times 9 =$ ▨
48. $4 \times 4 =$ ▨
49. $8 \times 9 =$ ▨
50. $3 \times 9 =$ ▨
51. $0 \times 4 =$ ▨
52. $2 \times 9 =$ ▨
53. $3 \times 4 =$ ▨
54. $1 \times 9 =$ ▨

55. $8 \times 8 =$ ▨
56. $9 \times 7 =$ ▨
57. $3 \times 6 =$ ▨
58. $10 \times 7 =$ ▨
59. $8 \times 6 =$ ▨
60. $9 \times 8 =$ ▨
61. $6 \times 7 -$ ▨
62. $7 \times 8 =$ ▨
63. $5 \times 6 =$ ▨
64. $7 \times 7 =$ ▨
65. $6 \times 6 =$ ▨
66. $0 \times 8 =$ ▨
67. $8 \times 7 =$ ▨
68. $7 \times 6 =$ ▨
69. $4 \times 8 =$ ▨
70. $5 \times 7 =$ ▨
71. $6 \times 8 =$ ▨
72. $9 \times 6 =$ ▨

Show your answers on your paper or in your Activity Workbook.

▶ Checkup for Basic Division

1. 35 ÷ 5 = ☐
2. 40 ÷ 10 = ☐
3. 30 ÷ 5 = ☐
4. 16 ÷ 2 = ☐
5. 15 ÷ 5 = ☐
6. 45 ÷ 5 = ☐
7. 90 ÷ 10 = ☐
8. 25 ÷ 5 = ☐
9. 10 ÷ 2 = ☐
10. 5 ÷ 5 = ☐
11. 80 ÷ 10 = ☐
12. 40 ÷ 5 = ☐
13. 8 ÷ 2 = ☐
14. 18 ÷ 2 = ☐
15. 20 ÷ 10 = ☐
16. 6 ÷ 2 = ☐
17. 20 ÷ 5 = ☐
18. 12 ÷ 2 = ☐

19. 27 ÷ 3 = ☐
20. 10 ÷ 1 = ☐
21. 12 ÷ 3 = ☐
22. 21 ÷ 3 = ☐
23. 0 ÷ 3 = ☐
24. 6 ÷ 1 = ☐
25. 18 ÷ 3 = ☐
26. 15 ÷ 3 = ☐
27. 1 ÷ 1 = ☐
28. 30 ÷ 3 = ☐
29. 7 ÷ 1 = ☐
30. 9 ÷ 3 = ☐
31. 9 ÷ 1 = ☐
32. 6 ÷ 3 = ☐
33. 0 ÷ 1 = ☐
34. 3 ÷ 3 = ☐
35. 24 ÷ 3 = ☐
36. 8 ÷ 1 = ☐

37. 72 ÷ 9 = ☐
38. 24 ÷ 4 = ☐
39. 27 ÷ 9 = ☐
40. 81 ÷ 9 = ☐
41. 28 ÷ 4 = ☐
42. 20 ÷ 4 = ☐
43. 63 ÷ 9 = ☐
44. 32 ÷ 4 = ☐
45. 54 ÷ 9 = ☐
46. 16 ÷ 4 = ☐
47. 45 ÷ 9 = ☐
48. 36 ÷ 4 = ☐
49. 9 ÷ 9 = ☐
50. 8 ÷ 4 = ☐
51. 40 ÷ 4 = ☐
52. 18 ÷ 9 = ☐
53. 12 ÷ 4 = ☐
54. 36 ÷ 9 = ☐

55. 42 ÷ 6 = ☐
56. 18 ÷ 6 = ☐
57. 42 ÷ 7 = ☐
58. 64 ÷ 8 = ☐
59. 30 ÷ 6 = ☐
60. 49 ÷ 7 = ☐
61. 54 ÷ 6 = ☐
62. 24 ÷ 8 = ☐
63. 21 ÷ 7 = ☐
64. 72 ÷ 8 = ☐
65. 48 ÷ 6 = ☐
66. 56 ÷ 8 = ☐
67. 56 ÷ 7 = ☐
68. 36 ÷ 6 = ☐
69. 48 ÷ 8 = ☐
70. 63 ÷ 7 = ☐
71. 6 ÷ 6 = ☐
72. 35 ÷ 7 = ☐

Class Activity

▶ **Use the Target**

X	1	2	3	4	5	6	7	8	9	10
1	1	2	3	4	5	6	7	8	9	10
2	2	4	6	8	10	12	14	16	18	20
3	3	6	9	12	15	18	21	24	27	30
4	4	8	12	16	20	24	28	32	36	40
5	5	10	15	20	25	30	35	40	45	50
6	6	12	18	24	30	36	42	48	54	60
7	7	14	21	28	35	42	49	56	63	70
8	8	16	24	32	40	48	56	64	72	80
9	9	18	27	36	45	54	63	72	81	90
10	10	20	30	40	50	60	70	80	90	100

1. Discuss how you can use the Target to find the product for 5×8.

2. Discuss how you can use the Target to practice division.

3. Practice using the Target.

4. **On the Back** When using the Target, how are multiplication and division alike? How are they different?

Write your answer to the "On the Back" question on your paper or in your journal.

Dear Family,

Your child is learning math in an innovative program called *Math Expressions*. Your child will learn math and have fun by:

- working with different objects and making drawings of various math situations.
- working with other students and sharing problem-solving strategies with them.
- writing and solving problems and connecting math to their daily lives.

At the beginning of this unit, your child will be learning the basics of multiplication and division. One learning tool is the "count-by." Using fingers can help.

2s count-bys   2   4   6   8   10   12

- Multiplication is a fast way to count same-size groups: $2 + 2 + 2 + 2 + 2 + 2 = 12$ is the same as 6 groups of 2, so we can say $6 \times 2 = 12$. To find 6×2, we "count-by" 2 and raise 1 finger 6 times: 2, 4, 6, 8, 10, 12. The last number we say is 12, so we know that $6 \times 2 = 12$.

- Division is the reverse of multiplication: $6 \times 2 = 12$ written as division is $12 \div 2 = 6$ or $12 \div 6 = 2$. To find $12 \div 2$, we "count-by" 2 up to 12 and keep track of how many fingers we raise. We raise 6 fingers to get to 12, so we know that $12 \div 2 = 6$.

It is vital that your child learn the basic multiplications and divisions. He or she must have a regular time and quiet place for practice every night.

Sincerely,
Your child's teacher

Your teacher will give you a copy of this letter.

Estimada familia:

Su niño está aprendiendo matemáticas con un programa innovador llamado *Math Expressions*. Su niño aprenderá matemáticas y se divertirá mientras:

- trabaja con varios objetos y hace dibujos de problemas matemáticos.
- trabaja con otros estudiantes y comparte estrategias para resolver problemas.
- escribe y resuelve problemas, y los relaciona con su vida diaria.

Al principio de esta unidad su niño aprenderá las reglas básicas de la multiplicación y de la división. Una buena herramienta de aprendizaje es "contar de cierto número en cierto número." Su niño puede usar los dedos para ayudarse.

contar de 2 en 2   2   4   6   8   10   12

- La multiplicación es una manera rápida de contar grupos del mismo tamaño: $2 + 2 + 2 + 2 + 2 + 2 = 12$ es lo mismo que 6 grupos de 2, entonces podemos decir $6 \times 2 = 12$. Para hallar 6×2 contamos de 2 en 2 y levantamos un dedo 6 veces: 2, 4, 6, 8, 10, 12. El último número que decimos es 12, por lo tanto sabemos que $6 \times 2 = 12$.

- La división es lo contrario de la multiplicación: $6 \times 2 = 12$, escrito como división es $12 \div 2 = 6$ ó $12 \div 6 = 2$. Para hallar $12 \div 2$, contamos de 2 en 2 hasta el 12 y observamos cuántos dedos levantamos. Para llegar a 12 levantamos 6 dedos, por lo tanto sabemos que $12 \div 2 = 6$.

Es importante que su niño aprenda las multiplicaciones y divisiones básicas. Debe tener un horario y un lugar tranquilo para practicar todas las noches.

Atentamente,
El maestro de su niño

Tu maestro te dará una copia de esta carta.

Vocabulary
equation

► Look at a Product in Four Ways

David picked some apples. He could have counted them one by one, but he thought he could use multiplication to count them faster.

He arranged the apples in four different ways, and found the same total each time.

Write a multiplication equation to represent each picture.

1.

2.

3.

4.

5. You have learned that multiplication is a way of finding the total in equal groups. Can you see or make equal groups in all four pictures? Explain.

▶ Introduce Arrays

Vocabulary

array

An **array** is an arrangement of objects in rows and columns. Each row has the same number of items, and each column has the same number of items. This array has 2 rows and 6 columns. We say it is a 2-by-6 array.

6 columns

2 rows •••••• 2 by 6 array
       ••••••

6. Write a multiplication equation for this array.

Make a drawing to show each array and then write a multiplication equation to represent the total number of objects.

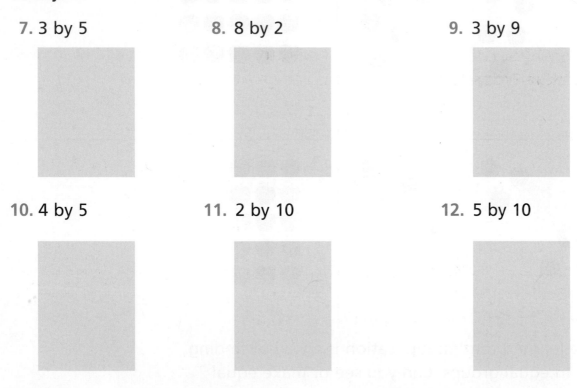

7. 3 by 5

8. 8 by 2

9. 3 by 9

10. 4 by 5

11. 2 by 10

12. 5 by 10

13. **Math Journal** The total number of objects is 18. Make two different arrays showing this total. Then write a multiplication equation for each array.

Arrays and Commutativity

Vocabulary

Commutative Property of Multiplication

► Commutativity with Arrays and Groups

The **Commutative Property of Multiplication** states that changing the order of the factors in a multiplication problem does not change the product. So, for any numbers *a* and *b*, the Commutative Property states that $a \times b = b \times a$.

14. How do these arrays show the Commutative Property for 2×3?

15. Explain how you could use arrays to show the Commutative Property for any two whole number factors.

16. On page 11, David arranged his groups of apples to form arrays. Do you think you could always arrange same-size groups to form arrays? Why or why not?

17. Is the Commutative Property true for repeated groups situations? Why or why not?

▶ Discuss Array Problems

Make a math drawing for each problem and then solve.

Show your work on your paper or in your journal.

18. Avi arranged her bottle cap collection into an array. The array had 4 rows with 9 bottle caps in each row. How many bottle caps are in her collection?

19. On one wall of an art gallery, photographs were arranged in 2 rows with 7 photographs in each row. How many total photographs were on the wall?

On a separate sheet of paper, write the answers to exercises 20–22.

20. In Lesson 1, you explored the relationship between division and multiplication. You saw that dividing means finding an unknown factor. Use this idea to explain what division is in an array situation.

▶ Write Division Problems

21. Write and solve two division word problems that are related to the multiplication word problem in problem 18.

22. Write and solve two division word problems that are related to the multiplication word problem in problem 19.

4 Class Activity

Show your answers on your paper or in your Activity Workbook.

▶ Checkup A: 2s, 5s, 9s, 10s

1. 3 × 2 =

2. 1 • 5 =

3. 8 * 5 =

4. 9 × 3 =

5. 5 • 2 =

6. 9 * 9 =

7. 8 × 2 =

8. 10 • 4 =

9. 7 * 5 =

10. 1 × 10 =

11. 10 • 6 =

12. 5 * 4 =

13. 9 × 7 =

14. 5 • 6 =

15. 2 * 1 =

16. 6 × 9 =

17. 10 • 8 =

18. 2 * 6 =

19. 9 × 5 =

20. 2 × 2 =

21. 5 * 3 =

22. 10 × 2 =

23. 5 • 5 =

24. 1 * 9 =

25. 8 * 9 =

26. 2 * 4 =

27. 5 • 10 =

28. 4 × 9 =

29. 7 • 2 =

30. 10 * 3 =

31. 7 × 10 =

32. 9 * 6 =

33. 2 * 9 =

34. 10 • 9 =

35. 10 × 10 =

36. 7 * 9 =

37. 4 / 2 =

38. $\frac{5}{5}$ =

39. 8 ÷ 2 =

40. 9 ÷ 9 =

41. 50 / 5 =

42. 2)$\overline{20}$

43. 54 ÷ 9 =

44. 10)$\overline{10}$

45. $\frac{10}{2}$ =

46. 81 / 9 =

47. 20 ÷ 10 =

48. $\frac{70}{10}$ =

49. 5)$\overline{30}$

50. 80 / 10 =

51. $\frac{45}{9}$ =

52. 20 / 5 =

53. 2)$\overline{14}$

54. 60 ÷ 10 =

55. 2)$\overline{6}$

56. 10 ÷ 5 =

57. 9)$\overline{27}$

58. 40 ÷ 5 =

59. 18 / 9 =

60. 2 ÷ 2 =

61. 36 / 9 =

62. 16 ÷ 2 =

63. 5)$\overline{15}$

64. 63 / 9 =

65. 90 ÷ 9 =

66. 12 / 2 =

67. 35 ÷ 5 =

68. 100 / 10 =

69. $\frac{45}{5}$ =

70. 18 / 2 =

71. 9)$\overline{72}$

72. 25 ÷ 5 =

Class Activity

▶ Play a Game

Play *Quotient Match* with your partner.

Rules for *Quotient Match*

Number of players: 2 or 3
What you will need: Product Cards: 2s, 5s, 9s

1. Shuffle the cards. Put the cards, division side up, on the table in 6 rows of 4.

2. Players take turns. On each turn, a player chooses three cards that he or she thinks have the same quotient and turns them over.

3. If all three cards do have the same quotient the player takes them. If not, the player turns them back over so the division side is up.

4. Play continues until no cards remain.

5. The player with the most cards wins.

Your teacher will give you the Product Cards.

Fluency Day: 2s, 5s, 9s, and 10s

Class Activity

▶ Discuss Word Problems

Solve each problem.

Show your work on your paper or in your journal.

1. Ben arranged his soccer trophies into 3 equal rows. If he has 12 trophies, how many trophies are in each row?

2. How many sides do 8 triangles have altogether?

3. For the yearbook photo, the science club stood in 3 rows with 5 students in each row. How many students were in the picture?

4. Tickets to the school play cost $3 each. Mr. Cortez spent $27 on tickets. How many tickets did he buy?

5. Jess solved 21 multiplication problems. If the problems were arranged in rows of 3, how many rows of problems did Jess solve?

6. Last year, 6 sets of triplets were born at Watertown hospital. During this time, how many total triplets were born at the hospital?

▶ Pictographs

A **pictograph** is a graph that uses pictures to show data.
The pictograph below shows the number of CDs of each
type in Kyle's collection.

7. How many jazz CDs does
   Kyle have?   10

8. How many hip hop CDs does
   Kyle have?   16   +10
                      together

9. In all, how many jazz and classical CDs does Kyle have?
   14 together

10. How many more hip hop CDs than rock CDs does
    Kyle have?   10

Kyle's CDs	
Type	**Number of CDs**
Jazz	⦿ ⦿ ⦿ ⦿ ⦿ 10
Hip Hop	⦿ ⦿ ⦿ ⦿ ⦿ ⦿ ⦿ ⦿ 16
Rock	⦿ ⦿ ⦿ 6
Classical	⦿ ⦿ 4

⦿ = 2 CDs

The pictograph below shows the numbers of pizzas of
different sizes served last night at the Leaning Tower pizzeria.

11. How many medium pizzas did
    the restaurant serve?

12. How many large pizzas did the
    restaurant serve?

13. How many small and medium pizzas did the restaurant
    serve altogether?

Sizes of Pizza Served	
Size	**Numbers of Pizzas**
Small	🍕 🍕
Medium	🍕 🍕 🍕 🍕 🍕 🍕
Large	🍕 🍕 🍕 🍕 🍕 🍕 🍕 🍕 🍕
Extra Large	🍕 🍕 🍕 🍕

🍕 = 5 Pizzas

Class Activity

▶ Equal-Shares Drawings

Copy and complete each Equal-Shares Drawing. Then tell whether the number in the box is a factor or the product.

1.

2.

3.
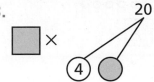

4.
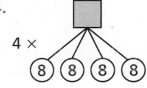

5.
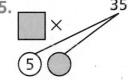

6.
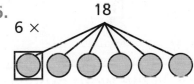

7. Make up word problems for the drawings in exercises 3 and 4.

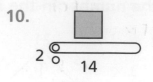
► Fast Arrays

Copy and complete each Fast Array.

8.
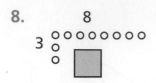

    8
  3 ○○○○○○○○

9.
       9
  □ ○○○○○○○○○
       45

10.
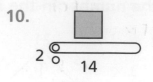

  2 ○
      14

11.
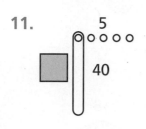

    5
  □ ○○○○○
    40

12.
  □
  ○○○○○○
  6 ○ 24

13.
     8
  ○○○○○○○○
  9   □

14. Write word problems for the drawings in exercises 8 and 12.

► Represent Multiplication With 1 and 0

Make a drawing to fit each description. Then write a
multiplication equation to represent the total number
of marbles.

1. 1 bag of 5 marbles

2. 5 bags of 1 marble

3. 0 bags of 5 marbles

4. 5 bags of 0 marbles

► Practice Multiplying 1 and 0

Find the product.

5. $1 \times 8 =$ ▪

6. $9 \times 1 =$ ▪

7. $0 \times 6 =$ ▪

8. $7 \times 0 =$ ▪

9. $1 \times 6 =$ ▪

10. $4 \times 1 =$ ▪

11. $0 \times 4 =$ ▪

12. $3 \times 0 =$ ▪

13. $1 \times 3 =$ ▪

14. $7 \times 1 =$ ▪

15. $0 \times 2 =$ ▪

16. $8 \times 0 =$ ▪

▶ Divide with 1

Draw a picture and write an equation to represent each situation.

17. 5 bagels are shared equally by 5 people.

18. 5 bagels are eaten by 1 person.

Look back at exercises 17 and 18. Replace each 5 with 4:

4 bagels shared by 4 people

$4 \div 4 = 1$

4 bagels eaten by 1 person

$4 \div 1 = 4$

19. Describe what you discovered. Can you make any general statements based on your discoveries?

▶ Practice Dividing with 1

Find the quotient.

20. $6 \div 1 = $ ▨

21. $8 \div 8 = $ ▨

22. $9 \div 1 = $ ▨

23. $3 \div 3 = $ ▨

24. $2 \div 1 = $ ▨

25. $1 \div 1 = $ ▨

26. $5 \div 1 = $ ▨

27. $4 \div 4 = $ ▨

28. $7 \div 1 = $ ▨

Class Activity

▶ Divide with 0

29. If 0 bagels are shared equally by 5 people, what is each person's share?

30. Write a division equation to show the situation.

31. Would you get the same answer if the 0 bagels were shared by a different number of people?

32. Can you make a general statement about dividing 0 things into any number of groups?

33. Is it possible to divide 5 bagels among 0 people? Why or why not?

34. What is the related multiplication problem for 5 divided by 0?

35. Can you find a factor that makes the multiplication equation true? Why or why not?

▶ Mixed Practice with 1 and 0

Find the product or quotient.

36. $0 \times 8 =$ ▪

37. $5 \div 5 =$ ▪

38. $1 \times 9 =$ ▪

39. $8 \div 8 =$ ▪

40. $6 \times 1 =$ ▪

41. $3 \div 1 =$ ▪

42. $0 \div 9 =$ ▪

43. $0 \times 2 =$ ▪

44. $0 \div 4 =$ ▪

45. $0 \times 0 =$ ▪

46. $7 \times 1 =$ ▪

47. $4 \times 1 =$ ▪

▶ Add and Multiply with 1 and 0

Solve each problem.

48. $5 + 0 = $ ▨

49. $0 + 1 = $ ▨

50. $7 + 0 = $ ▨

51. $5 \times 0 = $ ▨

52. $0 \times 1 = $ ▨

53. $7 \times 0 = $ ▨

54. Describe how you can remember the patterns for adding 0 and for multiplying by 0 so you won't get confused.

55. $5 + 1 = $ ▨

56. $1 + 2 = $ ▨

57. $7 + 1 = $ ▨

58. $5 \times 1 = $ ▨

59. $1 \times 2 = $ ▨

60. $7 \times 1 = $ ▨

61. Describe how you can remember the pattern for adding 1 and for multiplying by 1 so you won't get confused.

62. Write the two problems with the same answer.

$6 + 0$ $6 + 1$ 6×0 6×1

Class Activity

▶ **Checkup B: 2s, 5s, 9s, 3s, 4s, 1s, 0s,**

1. 5 * 3 = ▮
2. 1 · 5 = ▮
3. 9 × 5 = ▮
4. 9 × 3 = ▮
5. 4 · 8 = ▮
6. 8 * 3 = ▮
7. 8 × 2 = ▮
8. 10 · 4 = ▮
9. 7 * 5 = ▮
10. 1 × 10 = ▮
11. 81 / 9 = ▮
12. 5 * 4 = ▮
13. 9 × 7 = ▮
14. 5 · 6 = ▮
15. 7 * 4 = ▮
16. 6 × 9 = ▮
17. 10 · 8 = ▮
18. 2 * 6 = ▮

19. $2\overline{)6}$
20. 10 ÷ 5 = ▮
21. 4 / 2 = ▮
22. 40 ÷ 5 = ▮
23. 18 / 9 = ▮
24. 21 ÷ 7 = ▮
25. 36 / 9 = ▮
26. 16 ÷ 2 = ▮
27. $5\overline{)15}$
28. 90 ÷ 9 = ▮
29. 35 ÷ 5 = ▮
30. 0 / 10 = ▮
31. $\frac{45}{5}$ = ▮
32. 18 / 2 = ▮
33. $9\overline{)72}$
34. 25 ÷ 5 = ▮
35. 63 / 9 = ▮
36. 12 / 2 = ▮

37. $9\overline{)27}$
38. $\frac{24}{6}$ = ▮
39. 8 ÷ 2 = ▮
40. 9 ÷ 9 = ▮
41. 50 / 5 = ▮
42. $2\overline{)20}$
43. 54 ÷ 9 = ▮
44. $10\overline{)10}$
45. $\frac{15}{3}$ = ▮
46. 10 · 6 = ▮
47. 20 ÷ 10 = ▮
48. $\frac{70}{10}$ = ▮
49. $5\overline{)30}$
50. 80 / 10 = ▮
51. $\frac{72}{9}$ = ▮
52. 20 / 5 = ▮
53. $2\overline{)14}$
54. 60 ÷ 10 = ▮

55. 8 * 5 = ▮
56. 4 × 3 = ▮
57. 3 × 2 = ▮
58. 8 × 3 = ▮
59. 3 · 3 = ▮
60. 7 * 3 = ▮
61. 0 * 9 = ▮
62. 2 * 4 = ▮
63. 5 · 10 = ▮
64. 4 × 9 = ▮
65. 7 · 2 = ▮
66. 10 * 3 = ▮
67. 7 × 10 = ▮
68. 3 * 6 = ▮
69. 4 * 4 = ▮
70. 2 · 0 = ▮
71. 7 * 4 = ▮
72. 10 × 10 = ▮

▶ **Play a Game**

Play *High Card Wins* with your partner.

Rules for *High Card Wins*

Number of players: *2*
What you will need: Product Cards: 2s, 3s, 4s, 5s, 9s

1. Shuffle the cards. Deal all the cards evenly between the two players.

2. Players put their stacks in front of them, multiplication side up.

3. Each player takes the top card from his or her stack and puts it multiplication side up in the center of the table.

4. Each player says the answer and then turns the card over to check. Then players do one of the following:

- If one player says the wrong answer, the other player takes both cards and puts them at the bottom of his or her pile.
- If both players say the wrong answer, both players take back their cards and put them at the bottom of their piles.
- If both players say the correct answer, the player with the higher product takes both cards and puts them at the bottom of his or her pile. If the products are the same, the players set the cards aside and play another round. The winner of the next round takes all the cards.

5. Play continues until one player has all the cards.

Your teacher will give you the Product Cards.

Fluency Day: 2s, 3s, 4s, 5s, 9s, and 10s

Class Activity

▶ **Write Equations from a Factor Triangle**

1. Write eight equations based on this **Factor Triangle** .

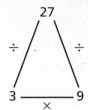

Show your work on your paper or in your journal.

▶ **Write Equations from a Fast Array**

2. Write eight equations based on this **Fast Array** .

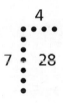

3. Draw a Factor Triangle and a Fast Array for $4 \times 6 = 24$.
   Then write the other 7 equations.

▶ Discuss the Relationship Between Multiplication and Division

4. Write your ideas about how multiplication and division are related.

Show your work on your paper or in your journal.

5. Explain how you can start with one multiplication or division equation and then write seven other equations.

Related Equations

9 **Class Activity**

Show your answers on your paper or in your Activity Workbook.

Class Sheet

1	2	3	4	5	6
7)‾3	7)‾4	6)‾0	1)‾6	1)‾3	1)‾0
4)‾2	1)‾8	6)‾1	3)‾6	2)‾4	4)‾1
5)‾3	6)‾4	10)‾0	4)‾10	5)‾0	9)‾3
3)‾1	2)‾3	5)‾4	2)‾0	10)‾4	3)‾7
4)‾0	1)‾4	3)‾8	4)‾3	3)‾2	6)‾3
1)‾2	1)‾0	9)‾4	1)‾7	8)‾1	3)‾3
4)‾5	10)‾3	4)‾7	9)‾0	4)‾9	8)‾3
3)‾4	4)‾6	1)‾5	2)‾1	3)‾9	4)‾4
9)‾1	5)‾1	3)‾5	1)‾9	3)‾0	1)‾10
7)‾0	3)‾10	7)‾1	8)‾4	10)‾1	4)‾8

Class Activity

Show your answers on your paper or in your Activity Workbook.

1

10)30

4)32

9)27

5)20

9)0

2)6

4)24

3)0

10)10

3)18

2

1)8

4)0

3)30

5)5

1)4

3)21

1)6

9)9

4)28

7)0

3

1)0

3)3

1)5

10)40

4)8

8)32

3)12

10)0

7)28

6)24

4

5)15

1)10

3)15

4)12

2)2

8)0

1)3

3)27

1)9

4)20

5

1)1

8)24

5)0

7)7

4)36

2)8

7)21

9)36

3)24

2)0

6

4)16

3)9

6)0

4)4

8)8

6)18

3)6

4)40

1)7

6)6

1	**2**	**3**	**4**	**5**	**6**
3 7)21	4 7)28	0 6)0	6 1)6	3 1)3	0 8)0
2 4)8	8 1)8	1 6)6	6 3)18	4 2)8	1 4)4
3 5)15	4 6)24	0 10)0	10 4)40	0 5)0	3 9)27
1 3)3	3 2)6	4 5)20	0 2)0	4 10)40	7 3)21
0 4)0	4 1)4	8 3)24	3 4)12	2 3)6	3 6)18
2 1)2	0 1)0	4 9)36	7 1)7	1 8)8	3 3)9
5 4)20	3 10)30	7 4)28	0 9)0	9 4)36	3 8)24
4 3)12	6 4)24	5 1)5	1 2)2	9 3)27	4 4)16
1 9)9	1 5)5	5 3)15	9 1)9	0 3)0	10 1)10
0 7)0	10 3)30	1 7)7	4 8)32	1 10)10	8 4)32

1	**2**	**3**	**4**	**5**	**6**
$10\overline{)30}$ — 3	$1\overline{)8}$ — 8	$1\overline{)0}$ — 0	$5\overline{)15}$ — 3	$1\overline{)1}$ — 1	$4\overline{)16}$ — 4
$4\overline{)32}$ — 8	$4\overline{)0}$ — 0	$3\overline{)3}$ — 1	$1\overline{)10}$ — 10	$8\overline{)24}$ — 3	$3\overline{)9}$ — 3
$9\overline{)27}$ — 3	$3\overline{)30}$ — 10	$1\overline{)5}$ — 5	$3\overline{)15}$ — 5	$5\overline{)0}$ — 0	$6\overline{)0}$ — 0
$5\overline{)20}$ — 4	$5\overline{)5}$ — 1	$10\overline{)40}$ — 4	$4\overline{)12}$ — 3	$7\overline{)7}$ — 1	$4\overline{)4}$ — 1
$9\overline{)0}$ — 0	$1\overline{)4}$ — 4	$4\overline{)8}$ — 2	$2\overline{)2}$ — 1	$4\overline{)36}$ — 9	$8\overline{)8}$ — 1
$2\overline{)6}$ — 3	$3\overline{)21}$ — 7	$8\overline{)32}$ — 4	$8\overline{)0}$ — 0	$2\overline{)8}$ — 4	$6\overline{)18}$ — 3
$4\overline{)24}$ — 6	$1\overline{)6}$ — 6	$3\overline{)12}$ — 4	$1\overline{)3}$ — 3	$7\overline{)21}$ — 3	$3\overline{)6}$ — 2
$3\overline{)0}$ — 0	$9\overline{)9}$ — 1	$10\overline{)0}$ — 0	$3\overline{)27}$ — 9	$9\overline{)36}$ — 4	$4\overline{)40}$ — 10
$10\overline{)10}$ — 1	$4\overline{)28}$ — 7	$7\overline{)28}$ — 4	$1\overline{)9}$ — 9	$3\overline{)24}$ — 8	$1\overline{)7}$ — 7
$3\overline{)18}$ — 6	$7\overline{)0}$ — 0	$6\overline{)24}$ — 4	$4\overline{)20}$ — 5	$2\overline{)0}$ — 0	$6\overline{)6}$ — 1

10
Class Activity

Vocabulary

Array
Repeated-Groups

▶ Identify the Problem Type

**Identify the type for each problem. Choose from this list.
(Write the letter, not the words.)**

   a. **Array** Multiplication
   b. Array Division
   c. **Repeated-Groups** Multiplication
   d. Repeated-Groups Division with Unknown Group Size
   e. Repeated-Groups Division with Unknown Multiplier
      (number of groups)

**For each multiplication problem, write a multiplication
equation. For each division problem, write both a division
equation and a multiplication equation.**

1. Latisha's uncle gave her 32 stamps and a new stamp
   book. The book has 8 pages, and she put the same
   number of stamps on each page. How many stamps
   did she put on each page?

   Problem type: ▨   **Equation(s):** ▨

2. A parking lot has 7 rows of parking spaces. Each row has
   7 spaces. How many cars can park in the lot?

   Problem type: ▨   **Equation(s):** ▨

3. Janine planted 5 rows of roses. If she planted a total of
   40 roses, how many did she plant in each row?

   Problem type: ▨   **Equation(s):** ▨

4. The produce market sells oranges in bags of 6. Santos
   bought 4 bags. How many oranges did he buy?

   Problem type: ▨   **Equation(s):** ▨

▶ Write Word Problems

5. **Math Journal** Write two word problems of different types.

Class Activity

▶ Repeated Subtraction and Division

Subtraction can be used to solve division word problems.

How many pieces of ribbon, each 5 centimeters long, can be cut from a ribbon that is 30 centimeters long?

6. What is the length of the ribbon?

7. What length will be cut off each time the ribbon is cut?

8. How many times did we subtract 5 cm from 30 cm?

9. How many pieces of ribbon, each 5 centimeters long, can be cut from a ribbon that is 30 centimeters long?

$$
\begin{array}{r}
30 \\
-5 \\
\hline
25 \\
-5 \\
\hline
20 \\
-5 \\
\hline
15 \\
-5 \\
\hline
10 \\
-5 \\
\hline
5 \\
-5 \\
\hline
0
\end{array}
$$

10. What division sentence can we write to represent this problem?

Show your work on your paper or in your journal.

Use any method to solve each problem.

11. How many pieces of ribbon, each 6 centimeters long, can be cut from a ribbon that is 18 centimeters long?

12. How many groups of 4 students can be formed from a group of 20 students?

13. How many pieces of string, each 4 centimeters long, can be cut from a string that is 36 centimeters long?

14. How many groups of 7 students can be formed from a group of 28 students?

Group and Array Word Problems

▶ Multiplication Strategies

These strategies will help you find 6×6:

Strategy 1: Start with 5×6, and count by 6 from there:

$5 \times 6 = 30$, plus 6 more is 36.

So $6 \times 6 = 36$.

Strategy 2: Double a 3s multiplication:

6×6 is twice 6×3, which is 18.

So $6 \times 6 = 18 + 18 = 36$.

Strategy 3: Combine two multiplications you know:

$4 \times 6 = 24$ 4 sixes are 24
$2 \times 6 = 12$ 2 sixes are 12
$6 \times 6 = 36$ 6 sixes are 36

1. Make a Fast Array or an Equal-Shares Drawing to show why Strategy 3 works.

2. Choose one of the strategies above. Explain how you could use it to find 7×6.

3. Choose one of the other strategies. Explain how you could use it to find 8×6.

Going Further

Vocabulary
function
rule

▶ Discuss Function Rules

A **function** is a mathematical rule. A **rule** can be made up of words, numbers, or words and numbers. "A ladybug has 6 legs" is an example of a rule.

A table can be used to show the relationship between the number of ladybugs and the number of legs.

ladybugs	1	2	3	4	5	6
legs	6	12	18	24	30	36

1. Explain how you could use the table to predict the number of legs 10 ladybugs would have.

2. How many legs do 10 ladybugs have altogether?

For each rule, copy and complete the table. Answer each question.

3. One nickel is the same amount of money as 5 pennies.

nickels	1	2	3	4	5	6	7
pennies	5	10	15	20			

4. How many pennies are equal to the value of 20 nickels? Explain how you know.

5. Each movie ticket costs $8.

tickets	1	2	3	4	5	6	7
cost	$8	$16	$24	$32			

6. What would be the total cost of tickets for a group of 15 people? Explain how you know.

Multiply and Divide With 6

Dear Family,

As your child continues to learn the basics of multiplication and division, he or she will bring home a variety of practice materials that are designed to help build fluency.

- **Target** This is a shaded overlay with a transparent L-shape and a circle. They are used together with students' multiplication tables. When the Target is placed over a multiplication table, the ends of the L show the factors, and the Target circle shows the product. Covering the product provides multiplication practice. Covering one end of the L provides division practice.

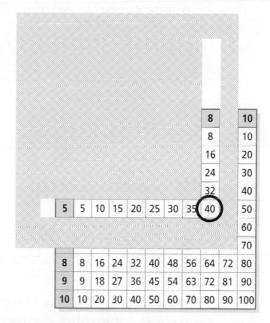

- **Write-On and Check Sheets** Students place Write-On Sheets in sheet protectors and try to solve various multiplication and division problems with a dry-erase marker. Students check their answers using Check Sheets.

- **Product Cards** Students first decide which side of each card will be facing up in their stack—multiplication or division. Students should choose the operation that is most difficult for them. After the student solves the problem mentally, he or she turns the card over to check his or her answer. Students should sort their Product Cards into *Fast, Slow,* and *Don't Know* piles.

Please provide a regular time and a quiet place for practice every night and keep the practice materials in a special place at home so your child does not lose them.

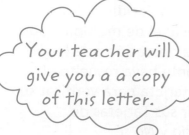

Your teacher will give you a a copy of this letter.

Sincerely,
Your child's teacher

Carta a la familia

Estimada familia:

A medida que aprendemos las reglas básicas de la multiplicación y la división, su niño llevará a casa una variedad de materiales de práctica que lo ayudarán a resolver estas operaciones con fluidez.

- **Objetivo** Es un acetato sombreado que tiene una zona transparente en forma de L y un círculo. Por lo general, se usa junto con las tablas de multiplicar de los estudiantes. Cuando el acetato se coloca sobre una tabla de multiplicar, los extremos de la L muestran los factores y el círculo muestra el producto. Se puede cubrir el producto para practicar la multiplicación. Se puede cubrir un extremo de la L para practicar la división.

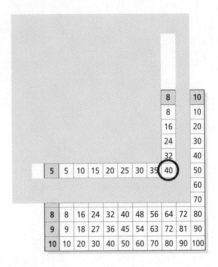

- **Hojas para escribir y comprobar** Los estudiantes colocan hojas para escribir sobre protectores de hojas y tratan de resolver varias operaciones de multiplicación y división con un marcador de agua. Los estudiantes comprueban las respuestas usando las Hojas para comprobar.

- **Tarjetas de productos** Los estudiantes deben decidir qué lado de cada tarjeta estará boca arriba en la pila; el de multiplicación o el de división. Es preferible que elijan la operación que les resulte más difícil. Una vez que el estudiante haya resuelto el problema mentalmente, dará vuelta a la tarjeta para verificar su respuesta. Los estudiantes deben clasificar sus Tarjetas de productos en tres grupos: *Rápido, Despacio* y *No sé.*

Por favor establezca un horario y un lugar tranquilo para que el niño practique cada noche y guarde los materiales en un lugar específico para que el niño no los pierda.

Tu maestro te dará una copia de esta carta.

Atentamente,
El maestro de su niño

Multiply and Divide With 6

Class Activity

▶ Use Multiplication Strategies

Read the letter. Help the Puzzled Penguin by answering the question.

Dear Math Students:

Today I had to find 8 × 7. I didn't know the answer, but I figured it out by combining two multiplications I did know:

$$5 \times 3 = 15$$
$$3 \times 4 = 12$$
$$\overline{8 \times 7 = 27}$$

Is my answer right? If not, please help me understand why it is wrong.

Thank you,

Puzzled Penguin

Show your work on your paper or in your journal.

▶ Solve and Discuss

Show your work on your paper or in your journal.

Solve each problem.

1. Julian arranged his swimming trophies on the 8 shelves above his dresser. He put 7 trophies on each shelf. How many trophies does he have?

2. Six students from Maile's class baked cakes for their school's cakewalk fundraiser. They each brought 6 cakes. How many cakes were there in all?

3. Roberto has an orchard with 48 peach trees. They are planted in 6 rows. How many columns of peach trees are in his orchard?

4. Kyle has 8 friends who would like to start an ant farm like his. He took 64 ants from his farm and divided them equally into 8 containers for his friends. How many ants will each friend receive?

5. Frances decides to sell her model airplane collection at her family's yard sale. She arranges her model planes on a table. She puts them in 6 rows, with 7 planes in each row. How many planes does she have for sale?

6. Tamara has just harvested the garlic she planted last fall. She has 49 heads of garlic. She plans to braid them into 7 equal bunches to use as gifts. How many heads of garlic will be in each bunch?

► Target Practice A

×	1	2	3	5	4	8	6	9	10	7
4	4	8	12	20	16	32	24	36	40	28
1	1	2	3	5	4	8	6	9	10	7
5	5	10	15	25	20	40	30	45	50	35
2	2	4	6	10	8	16	12	18	20	14
3	3	6	9	15	12	24	18	27	30	21
10	10	20	30	50	40	80	60	90	100	70
6	6	12	18	30	24	48	36	54	60	42
9	9	18	27	45	36	72	54	81	90	63
8	8	16	24	40	32	64	48	72	80	56
7	7	14	21	35	28	56	42	63	70	49

×	4	6	7	8
1	4	6	7	8
2	8	12	14	16
3	12	18	21	24
4	16	24	28	32
5	20	30	35	40
6	24	36	42	48
7	28	42	49	56
8	32	48	56	64
9	36	54	63	72
10	40	60	70	80

×	9	4	8	7	6	7	9	6	8	4
6	54	24	48	42	36	42	54	36	48	24
7	63	28	56	49	42	49	63	42	56	28
4	36	16	32	28	24	28	36	24	32	16
9	81	36	72	63	54	63	81	54	72	36
8	72	32	64	56	48	56	72	48	64	32
6	54	24	48	42	36	42	54	36	48	24
9	81	36	72	63	54	63	81	54	72	36
8	72	32	64	56	48	56	72	48	64	32
7	63	28	56	49	42	49	63	42	56	28
4	36	16	32	28	24	28	36	24	32	16

×	4	6	7	8
3	12	18	21	24
2	8	12	14	16
5	20	30	35	40
1	4	6	7	8
4	16	24	28	32
8	32	48	56	64
10	40	60	70	80
7	28	42	49	56
6	24	36	42	48
9	36	54	63	72

▶ Target Practice B

×	2	6	8	5	10	9	4	7	3	1
7	14	42	56	35	70	63	28	49	21	7
8	16	48	64	40	80	72	32	56	24	8
4	8	24	32	20	40	36	16	28	12	4
9	18	54	72	45	90	81	36	63	27	9
6	12	36	48	30	60	54	24	42	18	6
4	8	24	32	20	40	36	16	28	12	4
6	12	36	48	30	60	54	24	42	18	6
9	18	54	72	45	90	81	36	63	27	9
7	14	42	56	35	70	63	28	49	21	7
8	16	48	64	40	80	72	32	56	24	8

×	6	9	8	7	4
7	42	63	56	49	28
8	48	72	64	56	32
4	24	36	32	28	16
3	18	27	24	21	12
6	36	54	48	42	24
10	60	90	80	70	40
5	30	45	40	35	20
1	6	9	8	7	4
9	54	81	72	63	36
2	12	18	16	14	8

×	7	4	9	6	8	7	9	4	8	6
4	28	16	36	24	32	28	36	16	32	24
7	49	28	63	42	56	49	63	28	56	42
6	42	24	54	36	48	42	54	24	48	36
9	63	36	81	54	72	63	81	36	72	54
8	56	32	72	48	64	56	72	32	64	48
9	63	36	81	54	72	63	81	36	72	54
6	42	24	54	36	48	42	54	24	48	36
8	56	32	72	48	64	56	72	32	64	48
7	49	28	63	42	56	49	63	28	56	42
4	28	16	36	24	32	28	36	16	32	24

×	6	7	8	4	9
7	42	49	56	28	63
8	48	56	64	32	72
4	24	28	32	16	36
9	54	63	72	36	81
6	36	42	48	24	54
8	48	56	64	32	72
4	24	28	32	16	36
9	54	63	72	36	81
7	42	49	56	28	63
6	36	42	48	24	54

▶ Practice with Factor Triangles

Fill in the unknown number in each Factor Triangle.

1.

42

÷   ÷

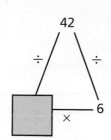   6
×

2.

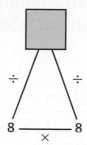

÷   ÷

8 —— 8
×

3.

56

÷   ÷

8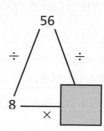
×

4.

72

÷   ÷

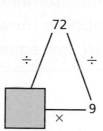   9
×

5.

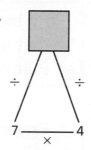

÷   ÷

7 —— 4
×

6.

30

÷   ÷

5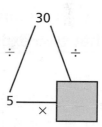
×

7.

49

÷   ÷

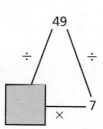   7
×

8.

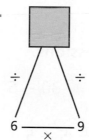

÷   ÷

6 —— 9
×

9.

63

÷   ÷

7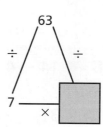
×

10.

21

÷   ÷

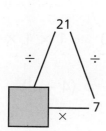   7
×

11.

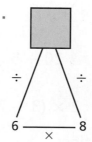

÷   ÷

6 —— 8
×

12.

36

÷   ÷

9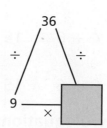
×

Going Further

▶ Expressions and Inequalities

In mathematics, an **expression** may use numbers, operations, and variables to represent an amount. All of these numerical expressions represent the number 6.

$$1 + 2 + 3 \qquad 10 - 4 \qquad 12 \div 2 \qquad 2 \times 3 \qquad 2 \times (2 + 1)$$

A **number sentence** describes how numbers or expressions are related to each other using the symbols =, <, or >. There are two kinds of number sentences.

An **equation** is a number sentence that uses an equals sign (=) to show that two expressions are equal. Example: $13 - 1 = 2 \times 6$	An **inequality** is a number sentence that uses a < or > symbol to show that two expressions are not equal. Example: $2 + 8 < 3 \times 4$

▶ Simplify and Compare

Write <, >, or = to compare the expressions.

1. $5 + 8 \quad\blacksquare\quad 14 - 4$

2. $30 \div 5 \quad\blacksquare\quad 30 - 5$

3. $3 + 6 + 0 \quad\blacksquare\quad 5 \times 2$

4. $7 \quad\blacksquare\quad 4 \times 3$

5. $4 \times 5 \quad\blacksquare\quad 5 + 5 + 5$

6. $7 + 5 + 3 \quad\blacksquare\quad 3 \times 5$

7. $18 - 9 \quad\blacksquare\quad 20 \div 4$

8. $6 + 3 \quad\blacksquare\quad 3 \times 6$

9. $25 \quad\blacksquare\quad 2 \times 10$

10. $2 + 4 + 6 \quad\blacksquare\quad 15$

11. $20 + 5 \quad\blacksquare\quad 20 \div 5$

12. $1 \times 10 \quad\blacksquare\quad 1 \times 1 \times 0$

13. $4 + 0 + 6 \quad\blacksquare\quad 15 \times 1$

14. $6 \cdot 4 \quad\blacksquare\quad 2 \times (3 + 7)$

15. $3 \times 0 \quad\blacksquare\quad (4 + 2) - 5$

Write two equations and two inequalities.

Fluency Day

Vocabulary

square array
square numbers

▶ Equations for Square Arrays

Write an equation to show the total number of dots in each **square array**.

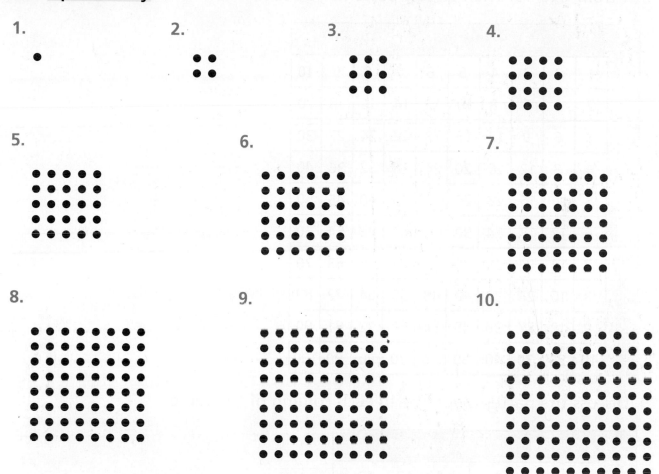

1.

2.

3.

4.

5.

6.

7.

8.

9.

10.

The products in exercises 1–10 are **square numbers**. A square number is the product of a whole number and itself. So, if *n* is a whole number, $n \times n$ is a square number.

▶ Find a Pattern

11. **Challenge** Describe the pattern in the number of dots added from one square array to the next.

Show your work on your paper or in your Activity Workbook.

▶ Patterns in the Multiplication Table

12. In the table, circle the product $n \times n$ for every value of n from 1 to 10. Then discuss patterns you see.

×	1	2	3	4	5	6	7	8	9	10
1	1	2	3	4	5	6	7	8	9	10
2	2	4	6	8	10	12	14	16	18	20
3	3	6	9	12	15	18	21	24	27	30
4	4	8	12	16	20	24	28	32	36	40
5	5	10	15	20	25	30	35	40	45	50
6	6	12	18	24	30	36	42	48	54	60
7	7	14	21	28	35	42	49	56	63	70
8	8	16	24	32	40	48	56	64	72	80
9	9	18	27	36	45	54	63	72	81	90
10	10	20	30	40	50	60	70	80	90	100

13. Discuss the patterns you see in each column of the table.

×	11	12
1	$1 \times 11 = \mathbf{11}$	$1 \times 12 = \mathbf{12}$
2	$2 \times 11 = \mathbf{22}$	$2 \times 12 = \mathbf{24}$
3	$3 \times 11 = \mathbf{33}$	$3 \times 12 = \mathbf{36}$
4	$4 \times 11 = \mathbf{44}$	$4 \times 12 = \mathbf{48}$
5	$5 \times 11 = \mathbf{55}$	$5 \times 12 = \mathbf{60}$
6	$6 \times 11 = \mathbf{66}$	$6 \times 12 = \mathbf{72}$
7	$7 \times 11 = \mathbf{77}$	$7 \times 12 = \mathbf{84}$
8	$8 \times 11 = \mathbf{88}$	$8 \times 12 = \mathbf{96}$
9	$9 \times 11 = \mathbf{99}$	$9 \times 12 = \mathbf{108}$
10	$10 \times 11 = \mathbf{110}$	$10 \times 12 = \mathbf{120}$

Square Numbers, 11s and 12s

Show your answers on your paper or in your Activity Workbook.

1

$7\overline{)5}$

$6\overline{)2}$

$9\overline{)8}$

$8\overline{)1}$

$5\overline{)6}$

$2\overline{)8}$

$6\overline{)1}$

$8\overline{)6}$

$7\overline{)9}$

$4\overline{)4}$

2

$5\overline{)4}$

$10\overline{)8}$

$8\overline{)7}$

$4\overline{)6}$

$7\overline{)7}$

$9\overline{)7}$

$6\overline{)10}$

$9\overline{)4}$

$6\overline{)8}$

$7\overline{)1}$

3

$2\overline{)4}$

$6\overline{)5}$

$9\overline{)6}$

$2\overline{)6}$

$8\overline{)9}$

$7\overline{)2}$

$3\overline{)6}$

$8\overline{)3}$

$3\overline{)4}$

$8\overline{)0}$

4

$4\overline{)8}$

$1\overline{)7}$

$6\overline{)9}$

$8\overline{)5}$

$5\overline{)7}$

$3\overline{)8}$

$8\overline{)2}$

$6\overline{)6}$

$7\overline{)6}$

$8\overline{)10}$

5

$7\overline{)4}$

$3\overline{)7}$

$10\overline{)6}$

$1\overline{)6}$

$8\overline{)8}$

$7\overline{)0}$

$10\overline{)4}$

$2\overline{)7}$

$7\overline{)8}$

$6\overline{)0}$

6

$6\overline{)4}$

$1\overline{)8}$

$4\overline{)7}$

$7\overline{)3}$

$5\overline{)8}$

$10\overline{)7}$

$6\overline{)3}$

$8\overline{)4}$

$7\overline{)10}$

$6\overline{)7}$

15 Class Activity

Show your answers on your paper or in your Activity Workbook.

1

8)80

5)30

7)21

3)18

8)32

6)12

4)24

7)70

2)16

7)35

2

8)24

6)42

10)70

5)40

9)54

4)32

7)56

2)8

6)36

1)8

3

7)7

4)16

6)24

8)56

2)12

9)63

6)60

3)24

6)6

8)64

4

8)16

7)42

6)0

6)48

10)60

7)14

1)7

3)12

9)36

7)0

5

2)14

10)80

7)63

6)18

1)6

5)35

8)40

6)30

8)72

5)20

6

7)49

8)48

3)21

9)72

4)28

8)8

6)54

10)40

8)0

7)28

Class Write-On Sheet 2B

15 Class Activity

❶	❷	❸	❹	❺	❻
5 7)35	4 5)20	4 2)8	8 4)32	4 7)28	4 6)24
2 6)12	8 10)80	5 6)30	7 1)7	7 3)21	8 1)8
8 9)72	7 8)56	6 9)54	9 6)54	6 10)60	7 4)28
1 8)8	6 4)24	6 2)12	5 8)40	6 1)6	3 7)21
6 5)30	7 7)49	9 8)72	7 5)35	8 8)64	8 5)40
8 2)16	7 9)63	2 7)14	8 3)24	0 7)0	7 10)70
1 6)6	10 6)60	6 3)18	2 8)16	4 10)40	3 6)18
6 8)48	4 9)36	3 8)24	6 6)36	7 2)14	4 8)32
9 7)63	8 6)48	4 3)12	6 7)42	8 7)56	10 7)70
4 4)16	1 7)7	0 8)0	10 8)80	0 6)0	7 6)42

Class Activity

1	**2**	**3**	**4**	**5**	**6**
10 8)80	3 8)24	1 7)7	2 8)16	7 2)14	7 7)49
6 5)30	7 6)42	4 4)16	6 7)42	8 10)80	6 8)48
3 7)21	7 10)70	4 6)24	0 6)0	9 7)63	7 3)21
6 3)18	8 5)40	7 8)56	8 6)48	3 6)18	8 9)72
4 8)32	6 9)54	6 2)12	6 10)60	6 1)6	7 4)28
2 6)12	8 4)32	7 9)63	2 7)14	7 5)35	1 8)8
6 4)24	8 7)56	10 6)60	7 1)7	5 8)40	9 6)54
10 7)70	4 2)8	8 3)24	4 3)12	5 6)30	4 10)40
8 2)16	6 6)36	1 6)6	4 9)36	9 8)72	0 8)0
5 7)35	8 1)8	8 8)64	0 7)0	4 5)20	4 7)28

Class Check Sheet 2B

15 Class Activity

▶ Factor Triangles and Fast Arrays

Fill in the unknown number in each Factor Triangle.

1.
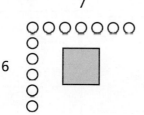

54 ÷ ÷ □ × 6

2.
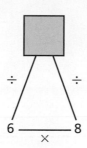

□ ÷ ÷ 6 × 8

3.
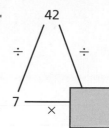

42 ÷ ÷ 7 × □

4.
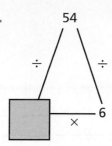

45 ÷ ÷ □ × 9

5.
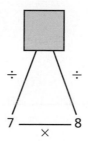

□ ÷ ÷ 7 × 8

6.
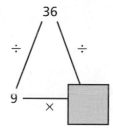

36 ÷ ÷ 9 × □

Fill in the unknown number in each Fast Array.

7.
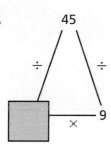

7
6 □

8.
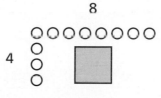

8
4 □

9.
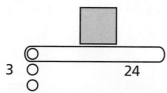

□
3   24

10.
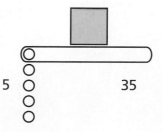

□
5   35

➡ **11. On the Back** Draw two Factor Triangles and two Fast Arrays. Then write a multiplication and a division equation for each.

Class Activity

▶ **Properties and Conjectures**

Vocabulary

Commutative Property of Multiplication
Identity Property of Multiplication

The **Commutative Property of Multiplication** states that you can switch the order of the factors without changing the product:

$a \cdot b = b \cdot a$ for any numbers a and b

The **Identity Property of Multiplication** states that the product of 1 and any other number is that number:

$1 \cdot n = n$ and $n \cdot 1 = n$, for any number n

---

1. Do you think there is a Commutative Property of Subtraction? That is, do you think $a - b = b - a$, for any numbers a and b? Test pairs of values to help you decide.

2. Do you think there is a Commutative Property of Division? That is, do you think $a \div b = b \div a$, for any numbers a and b? Test pairs of values to help you decide.

Use the Commutative Property of Multiplication to find the value of n.

3. $29 \times 8 = 8 \times n$ 4. $n \times 49 = 49 \times 16$ 5. $7 \times n = 36 \times 7$

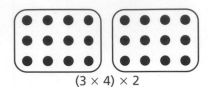

Vocabulary

Associative Property

▶ The Associative Property

6. How do these pictures show that $(3 \times 4) \times 2 = 3 \times (4 \times 2)$?

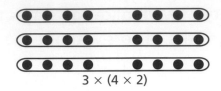

$(3 \times 4) \times 2$ $3 \times (4 \times 2)$

Find both products in each problem. Show how you got your answers.

7. $(6 \times 2) \times 3$ and $6 \times (2 \times 3)$ **8.** $(7 \times 5) \times 2$ and $7 \times (5 \times 2)$

The **Associative Property** states that the product is the same no matter how the factors are grouped:

$$(a \cdot b) \cdot c = a \cdot (b \cdot c), \text{ for any numbers } a, b, \text{ and } c$$

▶ Discuss the Distributive Property

Here are two ways to find the number of dots in this array:

- **Method 1:** First, add the number of gray columns and the number of black columns to get the total number of columns. Then, multiply the total number of columns by the number of rows.

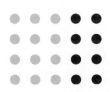

- **Method 2:** First, multiply to find the number of dots in each array. Then, add the results.

Notice that both methods give the same answer:
$4 \cdot (3 + 2) = (4 \cdot 3) + (4 \cdot 2)$.

Class Activity

▶ The Distributive Property

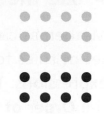

9. Find the number of dots in this array by adding the number of gray rows and the number of black rows and then multiplying by the number of columns. Fill in the blanks below to show this.

$(\blacksquare + \blacksquare) \cdot \blacksquare = \blacksquare \cdot \blacksquare = \blacksquare$

10. You can also find the number of dots in the gray array and the number of dots in the black array and then add the results. Fill in the blanks below to show this.

$\blacksquare \cdot \blacksquare + \blacksquare \cdot \blacksquare = \blacksquare + \blacksquare = \blacksquare$

11. Write a single equation showing that the two methods give the same answer.

$(\blacksquare + \blacksquare) \cdot \blacksquare = \blacksquare \cdot \blacksquare + \blacksquare \cdot \blacksquare$

The **Distributive Property** states that multiplication *distributes* over addition:

$$a \bullet (b + c) = a \bullet b + a \bullet c \text{ and } (b + c) \bullet a = b \bullet a + c \bullet a,$$
for any numbers a, b, and c

Use the Distributive Property to rewrite the expression so that it has only one multiplication and one addition.

12. $6 \bullet 3 + 6 \bullet 4$

13. $2 \times 7 + 8 \times 7$

14. $4 * 6 + 4 * 3$

Use the Distributive Property to rewrite the expression as the sum of two multiplications.

15. $8 \bullet (2 + 4)$

16. $(5 + 4) \bullet 6$

17. $4 \bullet (7 + 5)$

Vocabulary

Order of Operations
expression
simplify

▶ Use the Order of Operations

Mathematicians have developed a set of rules for simplifying expressions. These rules are called the **Order of Operations**.

ORDER OF OPERATIONS

1. Compute inside parentheses first.

2. Multiply and divide from left to right.

3. Add and subtract from left to right.

$(4 + 5) \times 3$
$9 \quad \times 3 = \textbf{27}$

$(2 \times 4) \times (6 \div 2)$
$8 \quad \times \quad 3 \quad = 24$

$4 + 5 \times 3$
$4 + 15 = \textbf{19}$

$10 - 12 \div 2$
$10 - \quad 6 \quad = \textbf{4}$

When parentheses are present, perform the operations inside parentheses first.

When parentheses are not present, multiply or divide before adding or subtracting.

**Rewrite each expression using • instead of ×.
Then simplify each expression.**

18. $6 \times 4 - 4$

19. $6 \times (4 - 4)$

20. $8 + 2 \times 7$

21. $(3 + 4) \times 6$

22. $(6 \times 3) - (2 \times 5)$

23. $2 \times (6 - 2) \times 5$

24. $5 + 3 \times 4$

25. $(3 + 4) \times (7 - 2)$

26. $18 \div 6 - 3$

Properties of Multiplication

Show your answers on your paper or in your Activity Workbook.

▶ **Checkup C: 3s, 4s, 6s, 7s, 8s**

1. $8 \times 5 =$ ◻

2. $7 \cdot 1 =$ ◻

3. $4 * 8 =$ ◻

4. $6 \times 2 =$ ◻

5. $7 \cdot 7 =$ ◻

6. $8 * 9 =$ ◻

7. $4 \times 4 =$ ◻

8. $8 \cdot 9 =$ ◻

9. $4 * 4 =$ ◻

10. $3 \times 8 =$ ◻

11. $4 \cdot 9 =$ ◻

12. $4 * 3 =$ ◻

13. $8 \times 6 =$ ◻

14. $7 \cdot 4 =$ ◻

15. $7 * 8 =$ ◻

16. $6 \times 4 =$ ◻

17. $7 \cdot 3 =$ ◻

18. $6 * 9 =$ ◻

19. $4 \times 6 =$ ◻

20. $7 \times 2 =$ ◻

21. $6 * 3 =$ ◻

22. $4 \times 7 =$ ◻

23. $6 \cdot 10 =$ ◻

24. $8 * 4 =$ ◻

25. $7 * 6 =$ ◻

26. $8 * 8 =$ ◻

27. $4 \cdot 2 =$ ◻

28. $8 \times 7 =$ ◻

29. $6 \cdot 5 =$ ◻

30. $8 * 2 =$ ◻

31. $7 \times 9 =$ ◻

32. $6 * 6 =$ ◻

33. $1 * 4 =$ ◻

34. $6 \cdot 8 =$ ◻

35. $4 \times 5 =$ ◻

36. $6 * 7 =$ ◻

37. $80 / 10 =$ ◻

38. $\frac{9}{3} =$ ◻

39. $27 \div 9 =$ ◻

40. $15 \div 5 =$ ◻

41. $24 / 4 =$ ◻

42. $8 \overline{)72}$

43. $32 \div 4 =$ ◻

44. $7 \overline{)35}$

45. $\frac{12}{6} =$ ◻

46. $0 / 8 =$ ◻

47. $70 \div 7 =$ ◻

48. $\frac{21}{3} =$ ◻

49. $7 \overline{)56}$

50. $36 / 6 =$ ◻

51. $\frac{24}{8} =$ ◻

52. $16 / 2 =$ ◻

53. $4 \overline{)40}$

54. $4 \div 1 =$ ◻

55. $35 \div 5 =$ ◻

56. $32 / 4 =$ ◻

57. $2 \overline{)8}$

58. $54 \div 9 =$ ◻

59. $27 / 3 =$ ◻

60. $24 \div 6 =$ ◻

61. $21 / 7 =$ ◻

62. $42 \div 6 =$ ◻

63. $8 \overline{)40}$

64. $15 / 3 =$ ◻

65. $36 \div 9 =$ ◻

66. $49 / 7 =$ ◻

67. $12 \div 2 =$ ◻

68. $48 / 6 =$ ◻

69. $\frac{16}{4} =$ ◻

70. $63 / 7 =$ ◻

71. $8 \overline{)56}$

72. $40 \div 5 =$ ◻

Class Activity

▶ Read Tables

Johanna collected information about the type, weight, and lifespan of several dog breeds. Information like this is **data**. Johanna organized the data into a **table**. A table uses **rows** and **columns** to display information.

Dog Breed Information			
Breed	**Type of Dog**	**Average Weight (pounds)**	**Average Lifespan (years)**
Pug	Toy	16	13
Yorkshire terrier	Toy	5	13
Dachshund	Hound	24	11
Bloodhound	Hound	95	11
Boxer	Working	65	9
Great Dane	Working	115	7
Labrador retriever	Sporting	65	11
Cocker spaniel	Sporting	26	13
Dalmatian	Nonsporting	55	11
Boston terrier	Nonsporting	17	14
Australian cattle dog	Herding	44	11
German shepherd	Herding	80	12
Jack Russell terrier	Terrier	12	14
Bull terrier	Terrier	55	12

1. What is the average weight of a dachshund?

2. Which breed in the table has the shortest lifespan?

3. Which two dogs are sporting dogs?

4. What is the difference in average weight between a Great Dane and a Jack Russell terrier?

5. **Math Journal** Make up your own question about the information in the table. Answer your question.

Solve Word Problems With Tables

▶ Make a Table

6. Make a table with information about members of your group. One column should show information that is numbers. The other should show information that is words.

Student's Name	▢	▢
▢	▢	▢
▢	▢	▢
▢	▢	▢
▢	▢	▢
▢	▢	▢

7. Make up at least three questions about your table.

Show your work on your paper or in your journal.

Going Further

Show your answers on your paper or in your Activity Workbook.

▶ **Discuss Function Tables**

Functions can be shown in a table, a graph, an equation, or in words.

Vocabulary
function
rule

When a table is used to show a function, the rule is shown in words at the top of the table, and the input value *x* is in the first column. The output value *y* is in the second column.

The equation at the bottom of the table shows the **rule** in an algebraic way.

add 2 to *x*	
x input	*y* output
0	2
1	3
2	4
5	7
9	11

$$y = x + 2$$

▶ **Write Function Rules**

Above each table, write a rule in words. After completing the table, write an equation that represents the rule.

1.

x input	*y* output
1	5
2	6
3	▢
▢	8
5	9

2.

x input	*y* output
0	0
4	▢
8	24
6	18
▢	6

3.

x input	*y* output
▢	10
3	15
7	▢
5	25
▢	20

4.

x input	*y* output
4	12
1	▢
▢	8
9	▢
6	14

Solve Word Problems With Tables

Equal Groups

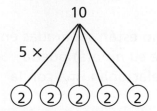

Dear Family,

Unit 1 of *Math Expressions* involves learning the skills that are needed to understand and represent multiplication and division situations, and solve real-world multiplication and division problems.

The operations of multiplication and division are not separated in this unit, but are studied together so that your child can see how the operations are related to each other.

Arrays and Area

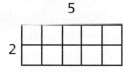

The kinds of multiplication and division situations your child will be working with are shown at the left. These situations include equal groups, arrays and area, comparisons, and combinations. Periodically throughout the unit, ask your child to explain the drawings and to tell you a word problem that represents each drawing.

Other topics of study in this unit include situation and solution equations, and tables and graphs. Your child will explore how to use situation equations to represent real-world multiplication and division problems and to use solution equations to solve the problems. Your child will also work with visual ways to display data, such as tables, stem-and-leaf plots, and double bar graphs.

Comparisons

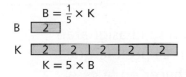

Throughout the unit, your child will also be assigned Practice, Homework, and Remembering activities. A number of these activities may need to be completed at home. Check to be sure that your child is completing any activities that are being brought home.

Combinations

	c	t	h	p	e
W	Wc	Wt	Wh	Wp	We
R	Rc	Rt	Rh	Rp	Re

Sincerely,
Your child's teacher

Your teacher will give you a copy of this letter.

Grupos iguales

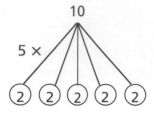

Estimada familia:

En la Unidad 1 de *Expresiones Matemáticas* los estudiantes aprenden las destrezas necesarias para entender y representar situaciones de multiplicación y división, y para resolver problemas de multiplicación y división de la vida real.

Las operaciones de multiplicación y división no están separadas en esta unidad, pero se estudian juntas para que su niño(a) pueda darse cuenta de cómo estas operaciones se relacionan una con la otra.

A la izquierda se muestran los tipos de situaciones de multiplicación y división con los que su niño(a) estará trabajando. Estas situaciones incluyen: grupos iguales, matrices y área, comparaciones y combinaciones. A través de la unidad, periódicamente, pida a su niño(a) que le explique los dibujos y que le diga un problema verbal como representación de cada dibujo.

Matrices y Área

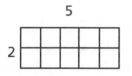

En esta unidad también se estudian otros temas, tales como ecuaciones de situación y solución, y tablas y gráficas. Su niño(a) explorará cómo usar ecuaciones de situación para representar problemas de multiplicación y división de la vida real y cómo usar las ecuaciones de solución para resolver los problemas. Su niño(a) también trabajará con formas visuales para presentar la información, tales como tablas, histogramas horizontales y gráficas de barras dobles.

Comparaciones

$$B = \frac{1}{5} \times K$$

B | 2 |

K | 2 | 2 | 2 | 2 | 2 |

$$K = 5 \times B$$

A través de esta unidad, a su niño(a) también se le asignarán Prácticas, Tareas y Actividades para recordar. Es posible que algunas de estas actividades se tengan que hacer en la casa. Asegúrese de que su niño(a) complete las actividades que trae a casa.

Combinaciones

	c	t	h	p	e
W	Wc	Wt	Wh	Wp	We
R	Rc	Rt	Rh	Rp	Re

Atentamente,
El maestro de su niño

Tu maestro te dará una copia de esta carta.

Vocabulary

combinations

► Complete and Interpret a Table

A restaurant makes veggie pizzas with 2 types of crust (thick or thin) and 5 toppings (pineapple, mushrooms, onions, green peppers, or black olives). You can use a table to show all the possible one-topping pizzas.

1. Copy and complete the table to show all the **combinations**.

	Pineapple	Mushrooms	Onions	Green Peppers	Black Olives
Thick	pineapple on thick crust	■	■	■	■
Thin	■	■	■	■	■

Look at the rows in the table.

2. How many one-topping pizzas have thick crust?

3. How many one-topping pizzas have thin crust?

4. What addition equation could you write to show the total number of one-topping pizzas?

5. What multiplication equation could you write?

Now look at the columns in the table.

6. For each topping, how many different pizzas are possible?

7. What addition equation could you write to show the total number of one-topping pizzas?

8. What multiplication equation could you write?

9. Math Connection Describe how finding the total number of combinations is like finding the total for an array.

Class Activity

▶ Create and Use Tables

On a separate sheet of paper, make a table to show all the possible combinations. Then write a multiplication equation to show the total number of combinations.

10. Rashawn has blue, green, red, and white T-shirts. He has black, blue, and tan pants. How many different outfits can he make?

11. A gift-wrapping service has 4 kinds of wrapping paper—plain, flowers, polka dots, and stripes—and 5 colors of ribbon—green, red, blue, yellow, and pink. How many different combinations of paper and ribbon are there?

▶ Use Any Method

Solve.

Show your work on your paper or in your journal.

12. Mr. Estrada has blue, white, gray, and pink dress shirts. He has a plain tie and a striped tie. How many different shirt-and-tie combinations can he make?

13. There are 8 girls and 7 boys in the school play. A boy and a girl will talk about the play at the school assembly. How many combinations of 1 boy and 1 girl are possible?

14. Joe's restaurant combines any pasta with any sauce to offer 18 combinations in all. If there are 3 types of pasta, how many types of sauce are there?

▶ Discuss Situation and Solution Equations

Read each problem and discuss how the equations relate to the problem.

1. Kaya put 28 apples into 4 equal packages. How many apples were in each package?

   Situation Equation: $4a = 28$

   Solution Equation: $a \times 4 = 28$ or $28 \div 4 = a$

2. A muffin tin holds 18 muffins. It has 6 muffins down one side. How many muffins go across?

   Situation Equation: $18 = 6m$ or $6m = 18$

   Solution Equation: $m \times 6 = 18$ or $18 \div 6 = m$

Write a situation equation and a solution equation, using a letter to represent the unknown. Solve your equations. Make a math drawing if you wish.

3. Five minivans took 40 students to the zoo. If each minivan had the same number of students, how many students were in each minivan?

   Situation Equation:

   Solution Equation:

4. Fifteen trading cards are arranged three equal groups. How many cards are in each group?

   Situation Equation:

   Solution Equation:

▶Write Situation and Solution Equations

Write a situation equation and a solution equation, using a letter to represent the unknown. Solve your equations. Make a math drawing if you wish.

5. Emilio bought 36 tomato plants for his garden. He can fit 9 tomato plants down one side of the garden. How many rows across will the garden have?

Situation Equation:

Solution Equation:

6. The bookstore owner says that she has 63 red pens. Sam sees 7 boxes of red pens, so how many red pens must be in each box?

Situation Equation:

Solution Equation:

7. A principal needs to purchase 35 rolls of ribbon to decorate the school gymnasium. If each package of ribbon contains 7 rolls, how many packages should the principal purchase?

Situation Equation:

Solution Equation:

8. The cafeteria has 7 tables down one side and 42 tables in all. How many tables go across the cafeteria?

Situation Equation:

Solution Equation:

9. The Crazy Paints store has 9 different colors of paint and 8 different styles of cups. How many different cups of paint could you make at the store?

Situation Equation:

Solution Equation:

Situation and Solution Equations

▶ **Discuss Comparison Problems**

To prepare for a family gathering, Sara and Ryan made soup. Sara made 2 quarts. Ryan made 6 quarts.

You can **compare** amounts, using multiplication and division.

Let r equal the number of quarts Ryan made.
Let s equal the number of quarts Sara made.

Ryan made 3 times as many quarts as Sara.
$$r = 3 \cdot s \text{ or } r = 3s$$

Sara made one-third as many quarts as Ryan.
$$s = \frac{1}{3} \cdot r \text{ or } s = r \div 3$$

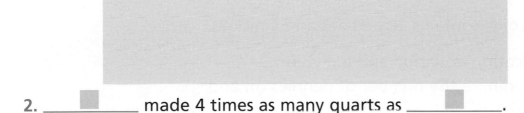

Solve.

Natasha made 12 quarts of soup. Manuel made 3 quarts.

1. Draw **comparison bars** to show the amount of soup each person made.

2. _____ made 4 times as many quarts as _____.

3. Write a multiplication equation that compares the amounts.

4. _____ made $\frac{1}{4}$ as many quarts as _____.

5. Write a division equation that compares the amounts.

6. Multiplication is the putting together of equal groups. How can this idea be used to explain why a *times as many* comparing situation is multiplication?

Class Activity

▶ Share Solutions

Solve.

In the gym, 8 girls are standing in one line and 4 boys are standing in another line.

7. Draw comparison bars to compare the number of people in each line.

8. Write a multiplication equation that compares the number of girls (g) to the number of boys (b).

9. Write a division equation that compares the number of boys (b) to the number of girls (g).

10. A collection of coins contains 20 pennies and 4 nickels.

    Write a multiplication equation and a division equation that compare the number of pennies (p) and the number of nickels (n).

11. A fourth grade class is made up of 12 boys and 24 girls. How many times as many girls as boys are in the class?

12. Fred has 24 football cards. Scott has $\frac{1}{6}$ as many football cards as Fred. How many football cards does Scott have?

Vocabulary

pictograph

▶ Use a Pictograph

A **pictograph** compares amounts. This pictograph shows how many books 5 students checked out of a library in one year.

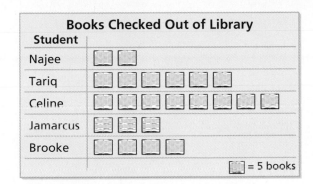

Use the pictograph to solve.

1. Write a multiplication equation that compares the number of books Tariq checked out (*t*) to the number of books Jamarcus checked out (*j*).

2. Write a division equation that compares the number of books Najee checked out (*n*) to the number of books Celine checked out (*c*).

3. Celine checked out twice as many books as which student?

4. Which student checked out $\frac{1}{4}$ as many books as Celine?

5. The number of books Dawson checked out is not shown. If Jamarcus checked out three times as many books as Dawson, how many books did Dawson check out?

6. **Math Journal** Write two sentences about the graph that contain the words *times as many*.

1–5

Class Activity

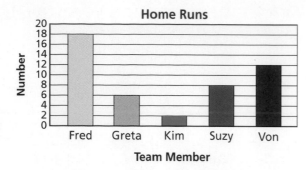

Vocabulary

vertical bar graph

▶ Use a Vertical Bar Graph

The **vertical bar graph** below shows the number of home runs hit by five members of a baseball team.

7. Write a multiplication equation that compares the number of home runs Suzy hit (*s*) to the number of home runs Kim hit (*k*).

8. Write a division equation that compares the number of home runs Greta hit (*g*) to the number of runs Fred hit (*f*).

9. How many times as many home runs did Von hit as Greta?

10. Which player hit $\frac{1}{6}$ as many home runs as Von?

11. This year, Fred hit twice as many home runs as he hit last year. How many home runs did Fred hit last year?

12. Write a sentence about the graph that contains the words *times as many*.

Show your work on your paper or in your Activity Workbook.

▶ Plan and Conduct a Survey

Choose a survey topic from the box or make up one of your own. Conduct your survey and record your results in the tally chart.

Topics
Favorite Fruit
Favorite Juice
Favorite Vegetable
Favorite Snack

Which _____ do you like best?	
Answer Choices	Tally

Use the tally chart to draw a horizontal bar graph.

Going Further

▶ Make a Stem-and-Leaf Plot

This table shows the heights in stories of some buildings in Chicago, IL.

Heights of Selected Buildings Chicago, IL (in stories)	
323 North Canal Street	37
115 South LaSalle Street	35
181 West Madison	50
350 East Illinois Street	58
10 East Ontario Street	49
1730 North Clark Street	35
205 North Michigan Avenue	44
1 North Wacker	50
325 South Wabash	45
69 West Washington	37
222 South Riverside Plaza	35
130 East Randolph	41

1. Write the heights in order from least to greatest.

2. Make a **stem-and-leaf plot** of the data.

Heights of Selected Buildings Chicago, IL (in stories)	
Stem	Leaf
■	■
■	■
■	■

Legend: ■

3. The building at 233 South Wacker Drive has a height of 110 stories. Explain how that height would be shown in a stem-and-leaf plot.

Mixed Comparison Problems

▶ Discuss Horizontal Bar Graphs

Discuss the **horizontal bar graph** with your class.

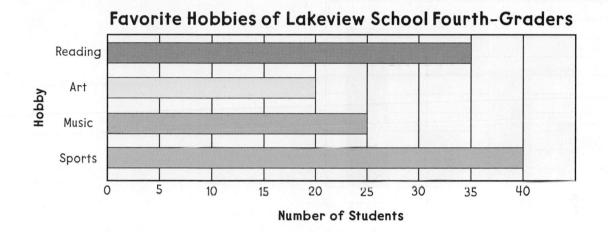

Favorite Hobbies of Lakeview School Fourth-Graders

Use the bar graph to answer the questions below.

1. How many fourth grade students said reading was their favorite hobby?

2. Which hobby is most popular?
   How many students chose it?

3. What hobby is half as popular as sports?

4. How many more students picked reading than art?

5. Altogether, how many students picked art or music?

6. Write your own question about the graph.
   Answer your question.

Class Activity

Vocabulary
vertical bar graph

▶ **Discuss Vertical Bar Graphs**

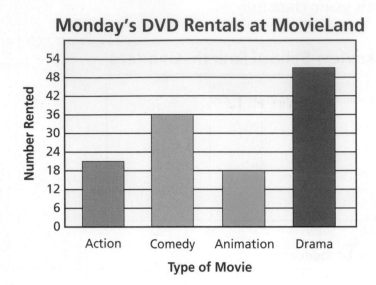

Monday's DVD Rentals at MovieLand

Number Rented / Type of Movie

Use the vertical bar graph to answer the questions below.

7. How many DVDs rented on Monday were dramas?

8. What was the least popular type of movie?

9. How many fewer animation movies were rented than comedy movies?

10. Is the total number of action and animation DVDs rented more or less than the number of drama DVDs rented? How much more or less?

11. What is the total number of DVDs rented on Monday?

12. Write and answer a question about the graph.

Class Activity

▶ Create a Bar Graph

Use the information in the table to create a bar graph.

Point Scored in Last Game	
Player	**Points**
Corey	6
Ming	18
Tamara	12
Hannah	10
Luisa	20

Things to Think About
- Will your bar graph be vertical or horizontal?
- Which axis will have the scale?
- What should the greatest scale value be? What should be the interval between scale values?
- What will the bars represent? How many bars will you have?
- How should you label the axes?
- What should the title be?

Going Further

Vocabulary

double bar graph

▶ Use Double Bar Graphs

The owner of a bike store wants to know how many of each type of bike she sells. She makes a **double bar graph** that shows the sales of each type for the last three years.

Answer each question, using the double bar graph.

1. In which year were the most mountain bikes sold? How many were sold that year?

2. In which year were the most road bikes sold? How many were sold that year?

3. In which year were the fewest bikes sold? How many bikes were sold that year?

4. In 2002, how many more road bikes were sold than mountain bikes?

5. In 2004, how many more mountain bikes were sold than road bikes?

6. **Math Journal** Make a double bar graph of some characteristic about boys and girls in your class, such as favorite color or favorite sport.

Show your work on your paper or in your journal.

Discuss Different Methods

Class Activity

▶ Discuss Multi-Step Word Problems

Solve.

Show your work on your paper or in your journal.

1. Eli reads 6 pages in a book each night. Shelby reads 8 pages each night. How many pages altogether will Eli and Shelby read in one week?

2. Min Soo is ordering 5 pizzas for a party. Each pizza will be cut into 8 slices. Three pizzas will have multiple toppings, and the others will be plain cheese. How many slices of plain cheese pizza is Min Soo ordering for the party?

3. Team A and Team B have 17 players each. Team A has 6 girls. Team B has twice as many girls as Team A. On both teams, how many players are girls? How many players are boys?

4. Jasmine and Mori each received the same number of party favor bags at a friend's party. Each bag contained 8 favors. If Jasmine and Mori received a total of 48 favors, how many party favor bags did they each receive?

5. In art class, Ernesto made some fruit bowls for his mother and brother. Nine apples can be placed in each bowl. Ernesto's brother placed 18 apples in the bowls he was given, and Ernesto's mother placed 36 apples in the bowls she was given. How many fruit bowls did Ernesto make?

6. On Tuesday, a bicycle shop employee replaced all of the tires on 6 bicycles. On Wednesday, all of the tires on 5 tricycles were replaced. What is the total number of tires that were replaced on those days?

▶ Solve Multi-Step Word Problems

Solve.

Show your work on your paper or in your journal.

7. Mrs. Luong bought 9 trees for $40 each. She paid for her purchase with four $100 bills. How much change did she receive?

8. Erica is painting the floors of her front porch and her back porch. The front porch floor is 10 feet by 6 feet and the back porch floor is 6 feet by 4 feet. How many square feet will Erica paint altogether?

9. Chan Hee is carrying a box that weighs 37 pounds. In the box are five containers of equal weight, and a book that weighs 2 pounds. What is the weight of each container?

10. A pet shop is home to 6 cats, 10 birds, 3 dogs, and 18 tropical fish. Altogether, how many legs do those pets have?

11. Dan has 7 fish in his aquarium. Marilyn has 4 times as many fish in her aquarium. How many fish do Dan and Marilyn have altogether?

12. Write a problem that is solved using more than one step. Then show how the problem is solved.

Class Activity

Show your work on your paper or in your Activity Workbook.

▶ Checkup D: 2s, 5s, 9s, 3s, 4s, 6s, 7s, 8s, 1s, 0s

1. 5 * 3 = ▢

2. 9 / 3 = ▢

3. 4)28

4. 6 • 6 = ▢

5. $\frac{81}{9}$ = ▢

6. 42 ÷ 6 = ▢

7. 7 × 9 = ▢

8. 18 / 9 = ▢

9. 6 * 7 = ▢

10. 2 • 8 = ▢

11. 8)32

12. $\frac{6}{3}$ = ▢

13. 24 ÷ 3 = ▢

14. 4 × 7 = ▢

15. 2 * 9 = ▢

16. 12 / 3 = ▢

17. 9)45

18. 5 • 6 = ▢

19. 1 × 8 = ▢

20. 7 * 4 = ▢

21. 16 ÷ 8 = ▢

22. 56 / 7 = ▢

23. 4)32

24. 0 • 3 = ▢

25. 9 × 8 = ▢

26. $\frac{12}{4}$ = ▢

27. 2 * 7 = ▢

28. 8 • 6 = ▢

29. 36 ÷ 9 = ▢

30. 3 × 8 = ▢

31. 54 / 9 = ▢

32. 9 * 7 = ▢

33. 8 • 3 = ▢

34. 4)36

35. $\frac{0}{7}$ = ▢

36. 48 ÷ 8 = ▢

37. 3 × 3 = ▢

38. 9 * 6 = ▢

39. 63 / 7 = ▢

40. 6)18

41. 8 • 4 = ▢

42. 6 × 3 = ▢

43. $\frac{63}{9}$ = ▢

44. 2 * 6 = ▢

45. 8 ÷ 4 = ▢

46. 3 • 4 = ▢

47. 30 / 6 = ▢

48. 7 × 7 = ▢

49. 7)42

50. 4 * 6 = ▢

51. $\frac{36}{6}$ = ▢

52. 6 • 8 = ▢

53. 27 ÷ 3 = ▢

54. 4 × 3 = ▢

55. 24 / 4 = ▢

56. 7)21

57. 2 * 3 = ▢

58. $\frac{40}{8}$ = ▢

59. 15 ÷ 3 = ▢

60. 27 / 9 = ▢

61. 8)24

62. 5 • 9 = ▢

63. 6 × 4 = ▢

64. $\frac{18}{3}$ = ▢

65. 64 ÷ 8 = ▢

66. 24 / 6 = ▢

67. 3 * 6 = ▢

68. 6)6

69. $\frac{20}{4}$ = ▢

70. 3 * 7 = ▢

71. 12 ÷ 6 = ▢

72. 9 × 9 = ▢

► **Factor Fireworks**

A **factor pair** for a number is two whole numbers whose product is that number. For example, 2 and 5 is a factor pair for 10.

A number greater than 1 that has 1 and itself as its only factor pair is a **prime number**. Some prime numbers are 2, 5, 11, and 23.

A number greater than 1 that has more than one factor pair is a **composite number**. Some composite numbers are 4, 12, 25, and 100.

The number 1 is neither prime nor composite.

Factor Fireworks show how a whole number can be broken down into a product of prime numbers. At the right are two Factor Fireworks for 12. This way of showing factors is also called a **Factor Tree** .

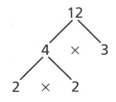

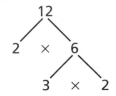

It doesn't matter how large a whole number is; you can always break it down into a product of prime numbers. At the right is a Factor Fireworks for 21,000.

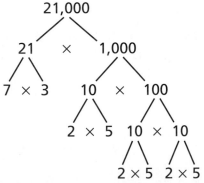

No matter what factor pair you start with, you will always get the same prime numbers at the ends of the branches. Below are three Factor Fireworks for 36. What 4 factors are at the bottom of each of these Factor Fireworks?

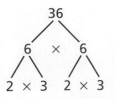

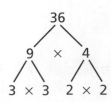

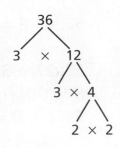

Factors and Prime Numbers

Class Activity

► Use Prime Factors to Divide

1. Make Factor Fireworks for the number 56.

2. Write an equation that shows 56 as a product of prime numbers.

3. Use your equation to help you find 56 ÷ 14.

4. Make Factor Fireworks for the number 72.

5. Write an equation that shows 72 as a product of prime factors.

6. Use your equation to help you find 72 ÷ 12.

Darnell said, "If you make a Factor Fireworks for an even number, you always have at least one 2 at the ends of the branches. If you make one for an odd number, you don't get any 2s."

7. **Math Journal** Experiment by making Factor Fireworks for a few even and odd numbers. Do you think Darnell is right? Explain.

Vocabulary

multiple

▶ Factors and Multiples

A **multiple** of a number is a product of that number and a counting number.

8. What are the first five multiples of 4? Explain your method.

9. Write the first ten multiples of 8.

10. Give two reasons why 21 is a multiple of 7.

11. One factor of 12 is 6. Five other numbers are factors of 12. What are those numbers? Explain how you know.

▶ Prime Factorization and Multiples

12. Write the prime factorization of 60.

13. Explain why 60 is a multiple of each factor you wrote for Problem 5.

14. Is 50 a prime number? Explain why or why not.

15. The product of 2 × 3 × 5 is 30. Describe two relationships that the numbers and the product share.

Multiplication and Division Problems

Class Activity

►Math and Science

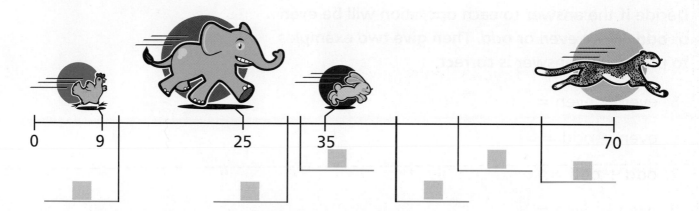

The fastest recorded running speed for a human is about 27 miles per hour over $\frac{1}{4}$ mile. The table below shows data for the estimated fastest running speeds for ten animals over the same distance.

Running Speeds	
Animal	**Estimated Speed**
Cheetah	70 mph
Pronghorn antelope	61 mph
Lion	50 mph
Zebra	40 mph
Rabbit	35 mph
Giraffe	32 mph
House cat	30 mph
Elephant	25 mph
Squirrel	12 mph
Chicken	9 mph

1. A human can run about how many times as fast as a chicken?

2. Which animal can run closest to the fastest recorded human speed?

3. Name an animal that can run faster than a squirrel but slower than a zebra.

4. Copy the number line at the top of the page. Write the missing animal names in the correct positions.

1–9

▶ Even and Odd Numbers

Decide if the answer to each operation will be even or odd. Write *even* or *odd.* Then give two examples to prove your answer is correct.

5. even + even = ▢

6. even + odd = ▢

7. odd + odd = ▢

8. even − even = ▢

9. even − odd = ▢

10. odd − odd = ▢

11. even × even = ▢

12. even × odd = ▢

13. odd × odd = ▢

14. When you divide 2 even whole numbers will the answer always be even? Use examples to support your answer.

Use the process of elimination to identify the product. Explain your choice.

15. 22 × 15

    A. 230   **B.** 233   **C.** 330   **D.** 333

    Using Mathematical Processes

Write an equation to solve each problem.

Show your work on your paper or in your journal.

1. Juan and Tina are making cracker snacks. They have 4 kinds of spreads and 7 food toppings for the spreads. They always use one spread and one food topping on each cracker snack. How many different kinds of cracker snacks can they make in all?

2. There are 36 desks in Jan's classroom. If there are 9 rows of desks, how many desks are in each row?

3. James has 35 cars. He can display 5 cars on each shelf. How many shelves will he use to display cars?

4. A car company has 15 combinations of outside and inside colors. For the inside they have black, tan, or gray. How many different outside colors do they have?

The bar graph shows the number of students in each grade at Central Elementary School.

5. Which grade has $\frac{1}{2}$ as many students as fourth grade?

6. Which grade has three times as many students as first grade?

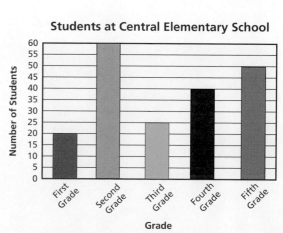

Students at Central Elementary School

The pictograph shows the number of pounds of fruits sold at a fruit stand.

7. Which fruit was sold twice as much as bananas?

8. Which fruit was sold $\frac{1}{4}$ as much as apples?

Pounds of Fruits Sold	
Fruit	**Pounds of Fruit**
Apples	🛍🛍🛍🛍🛍🛍🛍🛍
Bananas	🛍🛍🛍
Oranges	🛍🛍🛍
Pears	🛍🛍🛍🛍🛍🛍
Strawberries	🛍🛍🛍🛍🛍

🛍 = 2 pounds of fruit sold

9. Write the factors for each number and then identify the prime numbers.

   a. 63   b. 17

10. **Solve the word problem.**

   a. **Extended Response** Sam bought 7 hats for $6 each. He paid with a $50 bill. How much change did he receive? Explain how you found your answer.

   b. If you multiply two prime numbers will the product always be prime? Explain your reasoning.

Vocabulary

plane
congruent

▶ **Explore Congruence**

Sherrie used one side of a small box to trace two figures.

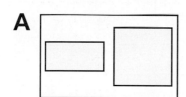 

1. Which picture shows her paper? How do you know?

A 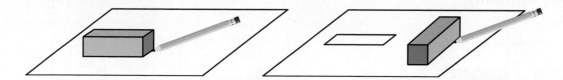 **B** **C**

Two-dimensional (2-D) figures are called **plane** figures.
They are **congruent** when they are exactly the same size
and shape.

2. Do the figures on Sherrie's paper look congruent?
Why or why not?

3. Which two figures look congruent? Explain how you know.

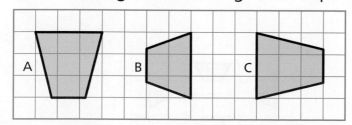

▶ Identify Congruent Figures

**Do all the figures in each group look congruent?
Explain your thinking.**

4.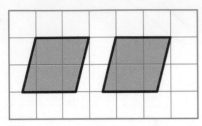

5.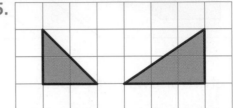

6.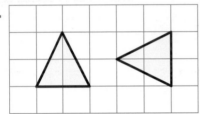

7.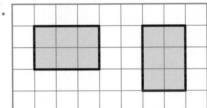

8.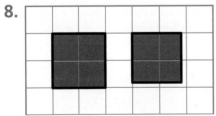

9.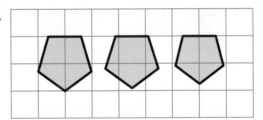

10.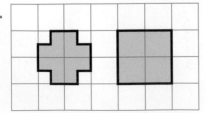

11.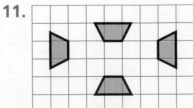

Congruence, Similarity, and Symmetry

▶ Discuss Similar Figures

Figures that are the same shape, but not necessarily the same size, are **similar** figures.

Look at the figures below.

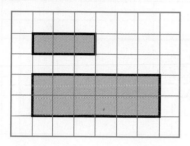

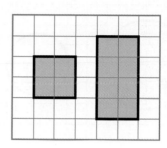

These figures are similar. They are the same shape. They are not the same size.

These figures are not similar because they are not the same shape.

Congruent figures are exactly the same size and shape. The figures at the right are congruent.

Congruent figures are also similar.

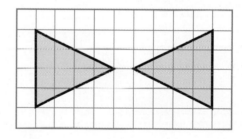

**Decide if each pair of figures appear to be similar.
Write *similar* or *not similar*.**

12.

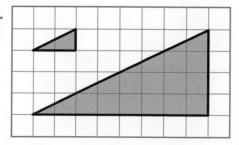

13.

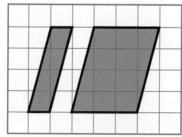

▶ Identify Similar Figures

Decide if each pair of figures appear to be similar. Write *similar* or *not similar*. Then decide if the figures appear to be congruent. Write *congruent* or *not congruent*.

14.

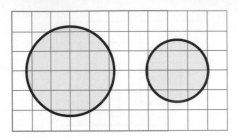

15.

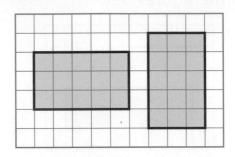

Write *true* or *false* for each sentence. Draw an example.

16. All squares are similar.

17. All right triangles are similar.

18. Draw two similar figures that are not congruent. Describe the measures of the figures, and explain why they are similar.

Congruence, Similarity, and Symmetry

Show your work on your paper or in your Activity Workbook.

▶ Identify Lines of Symmetry

A plane figure has **line symmetry** if you can fold it to make two parts that are mirror images. The fold is called a **line of symmetry**.

Does the figure have line symmetry? Write *yes* or *no*.

19.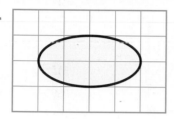

20.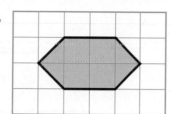

21.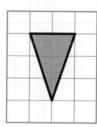

22.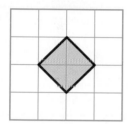

23.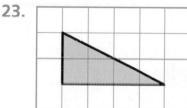

24.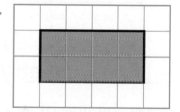

25. Which figures have more than one line of symmetry?

Draw the other half of each figure to make a whole figure with line symmetry.

26.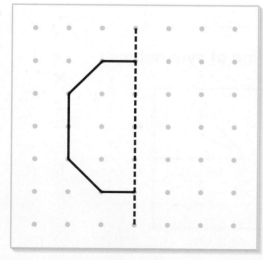

27.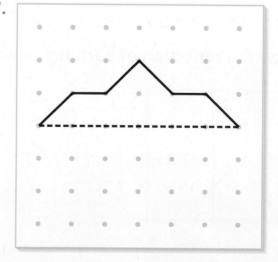

2–1

Going Further

Show your work on your paper or in your Activity Workbook.

Vocabulary

reflection

▶ Discuss Line Symmetry

A line of symmetry divides a figure into two congruent parts. The figure on one side of a line of symmetry is a *mirror image* of the figure on the other side. The mirror image is called a **reflection** because the line of symmetry is also a line of reflection.

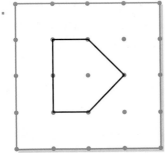
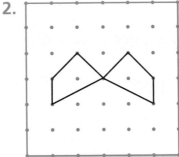

▶ Line Symmetry and Reflections

Draw the line of symmetry.

1.
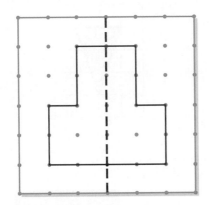

2.
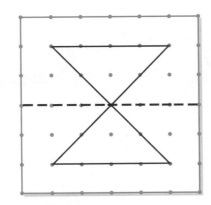

Draw the reflection of each figure across the line of symmetry.

3.
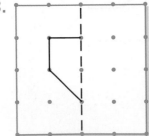

4.
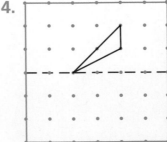

92 UNIT 2 LESSON 1

Congruence, Similarity, and Symmetry

Family Letter

Square
4 equal sides
opposite sides parallel
4 right angles

Rectangle
2 pairs of parallel sides
4 right angles

Rhombus
4 equal sides
opposite sides parallel

Parallelogram
2 pairs of parallel sides

Dear Family,

Your child will be learning about geometry throughout the school year. This first unit is about a group of geometric figures called quadrilaterals, which get their name because they have four (*quad-*) sides (*-lateral*). Four different kinds of quadrilaterals are shown here.

In this unit, your child will also learn the difference between perimeter and area. Area drawings help children to understand multi-digit multiplication.

For example:

$$4 \times 26 = 104$$

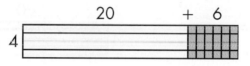

$$80 + 24 = 104$$

We urge you to encourage regular home practice of the basic multiplications and divisions. We will return to more of them in about a week. Later in the year, we will be learning about both multi-digit multiplication and multi-digit division.

If you have any questions or comments, please call or write to me.

Sincerely,
Your child's teacher

Your teacher will give you a copy of this letter.

Carta a la familia

Cuadrado
4 lados iguales
lados opuestos paralelos
4 ángulos rectos

Rectángulo
2 pares de lados paralelos
4 ángulos rectos

Rombo
4 lados iguales
lados opuestos paralelos

Paralelogramo
2 pares de lados paralelos

Estimada familia:

Durante el año escolar, su niño aprenderá geometría. La primera unidad trata de un grupo de figuras geométricas llamadas cuadriláteros, las cuales reciben este nombre porque tienen cuatro (*cuad-*) lados (*latero*). Aquí se muestran cuatro tipos diferentes de cuadriláteros.

En esta unidad, su niño también aprenderá la diferencia entre perímetro y área. Los dibujos de áreas ayudarán a comprender la multiplicación con números de más de un dígito.

Por ejemplo:

$$4 \times 26 = 104$$

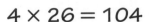
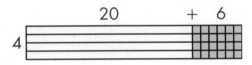

$$80 + 24 = 104$$

Recomendamos que anime a su niño a prácticar las multiplicaciones y divisiones básicas en casa. En una semana veremos más de éstas. Más adelante en el año aprenderemos a multiplicar y a dividir con números de más de un dígito.

Si tiene alguna pregunta o comentario, por favor comuníquese conmigo.

Atentamente,
El maestro de su niño

Tu maestro te dará una copia de esta carta.

Congruence, Similarity, and Symmetry

2–2

Class Activity

▶ **Sort and Name Figures**

Examine these figures.

A    B   C   D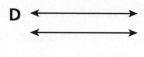

E 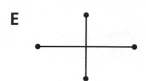   F    G   H

I    J    K   L

M 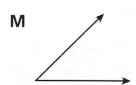   N 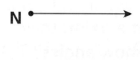   O   P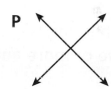

1. How are some of the figures alike?

2. How do some of the figures differ from one another?

Class Activity

Vocabulary

perpendicular
right angle
parallel

▶ Sort and Name Figures (continued)

Use the figures on the previous page.

3. A **line** is straight and continues forever in both directions. You can say that a figure is a line or you can draw arrowheads on its ends to say that it extends forever. Which figures show lines?

line

4. A **line segment** has a fixed length. If a figure is a line segment, it cannot be made longer. You can add points at the ends of the line segment to show that it cannot be made longer. Which figures show line segments?

line segment

5. A **ray** begins at a point and can go on forever, but in only one direction. Which figures show rays?

ray

6. When lines, line segments, or rays meet at a point, they form one or more **angles**. Which figures show angles?

angle

7. When two lines, line segments, or rays cross and form four congruent angles, the lines are **perpendicular** and the angles made are **right angles**. Which figures look perpendicular?

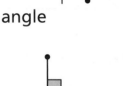

perpendicular line segments

8. When two lines are the same distance apart at every point they are called **parallel**. Which figures look as if the lines, rays, or line segments are parallel?

parallel lines

Vocabulary

vertex
angle

► Label Lines, Line Segments, Rays, and Angles

You can name figures by labeling them with letters.

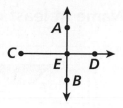

9. The letters *AB* name the line in this figure.
   Which letters name the ray in the figure?

10. A **vertex** is a point that is common to the two sides
    of an angle. One **angle** in this figure is ∠*AEC*. The
    middle letter of an angle's name indicates its vertex.

    Name three other angles in this figure.

**Name the line segments, vertex points, and angles
in each figure below.**

11.

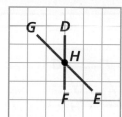

Line segments: ▨

Vertex point: ▨

Angles: ▨

12.

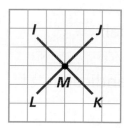

Line segments: ▨

Vertex point: ▨

Angles: ▨

13.

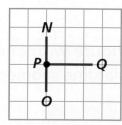

Line segments: ▨

Vertex point: ▨

Angles: ▨

14. Choose one of figures 11–13 and name the line segments
    and angles that look congruent.

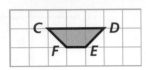

2-2

Class Activity

Show your work on your paper or in your Activity Workbook.

▶ **Label the Parts of Plane Figures**

For each figure, name the sides that look parallel and those that look perpendicular. Not every example has both. Name at least one angle.

15.

Parallel: ▪

Perpendicular: ▪

Angle: ▪

16.

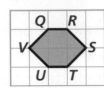

Parallel: ▪

Perpendicular: ▪

Angle: ▪

17.

Parallel: ▪

Perpendicular: ▪

Angle: ▪

18.

Parallel: ▪

Perpendicular: ▪

Angle: ▪

19.

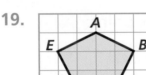

Parallel: ▪

Perpendicular: ▪

Angle: ▪

20.

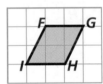

Parallel: ▪

Perpendicular: ▪

Angle: ▪

▶ **Draw Figures**

21. Draw and label a figure with one pair of parallel line segments.

22. Draw and label a figure with one pair of perpendicular line segments.

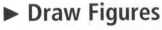

Lines, Line Segments, and Rays

▶ Describe 4-Sided Figures

José has a new puppy named Daisy. He needs to build a four-sided dog pen in his yard for her. He wants us to help him plan a pen for Daisy.

1. Which of these figures could be Daisy's pen?

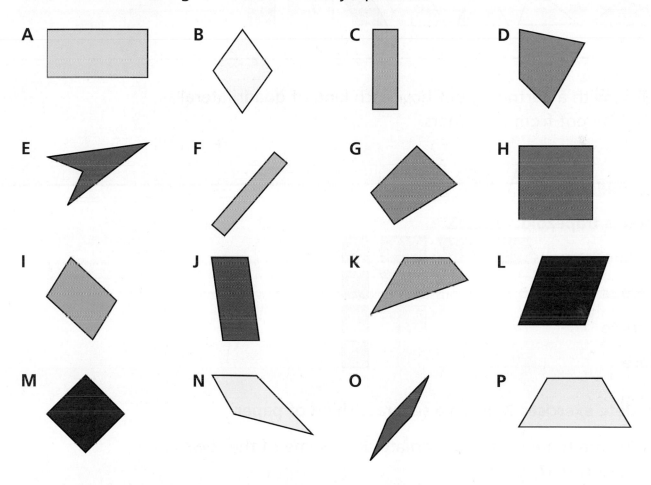

2. Which pens would Daisy probably like the most? Why?

3. Look at the sides and angles of all the figures. Which figures can we group together because they are alike in some way?

4. How are all the figures alike in some way? Explain your answer.

Class Activity

▶ **Discuss Quadrilaterals**

The prefix *quad-* means "four." The suffix *-lateral* means "sides."

Vocabulary

quadrilateral
trapezoid
isosceles trapezoid
parallelogram
rhombus

5. Why are all of these figures called **quadrilaterals**?

6. Talk with a partner about how each kind of quadrilateral is different from the others.

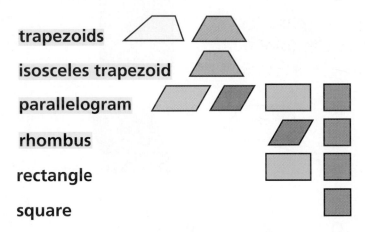

trapezoids

isosceles trapezoid

parallelogram

rhombus

rectangle

square

Complete exercises 7–10 on a separate sheet of paper.

7. Why are there several quadrilaterals in some of the rows in exercise 6?

Why is each sentence below true?

8. A rhombus is always a parallelogram, but a parallelogram isn't always a rhombus.

9. A rectangle is a parallelogram, but a parallelogram is not necessarily a rectangle.

10. A square is a rectangle, but a rectangle does not have to be a square.

▶ Units of Perimeter

The prefix *peri-* means "around." The suffix *-meter* means "measure." **Perimeter** is the measurement of the distance around the outside of a figure.

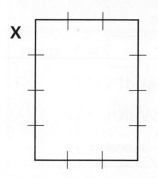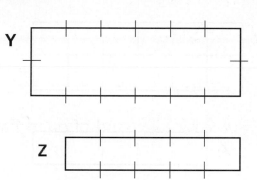

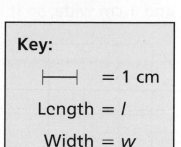

Key:

⊢———⊣ = 1 cm

Length = *l*

Width = *w*

Perimeter = *P*

Vocabulary

perimeter
unit
length
width

1. The measurement **unit** for these rectangles is 1 centimeter (1 cm). How can you find the total number of centimeters around the outside of each rectangle?

2. What is the perimeter of rectangle X? of rectangle Y? of rectangle Z?

3. What numeric method did you use to find each perimeter?

4. Look at the key: **length** is the distance across a rectangle and **width** is the distance up-and-down. Perimeter is the total distance around the outside. Use the letters *l*, *w*, and *P* to write a general equation for the perimeter of rectangles.

▶ **Units of Area**

Vocabulary

area
square units

Area is the total number of **square units** inside a figure.
Each square unit inside these rectangles is 1 cm long
and 1 cm wide, so it is 1 square centimeter (1 sq cm).

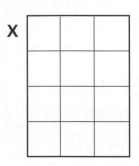

X

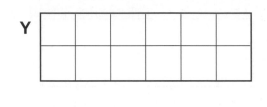

Y

Z

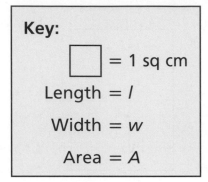

Key:

$\square$ = 1 sq cm

Length = l

Width = w

Area = A

5. How can you find the total number of square
   centimeters inside each rectangle?

6. What is the area of rectangle X? of rectangle Y?
   of rectangle Z?

7. Using l to stand for length, w to stand for width, and
   A to stand for area, what general equation can you
   write for finding the area of any rectangle?

8. Why does the same general equation work for
   all rectangles?

Perimeter and Area of Rectangles

▶ Discuss Real-World Situations

Solve and discuss the word problems.

9. Taci's father made an array of square tiles on the bathroom floor before gluing them down. How many tiles across did his array have? How many tiles up-and-down? How many in all?

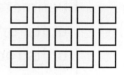

10. Taci wanted to know if the number of tiles in the array would be the same or different if her father took out the spaces between the tiles. What did her father tell her? Why?

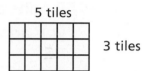

5 tiles

3 tiles

11. How does knowing about arrays help you to find the area of any rectangle?

12. The 15 tiles fit exactly in the bathroom without any spaces. If the measurement of one side of a single tile is 1 foot, what is the perimeter of the bathroom? What is its area?

13. If you know only the outside measurements for any rectangle, can you find its area? How? Why does this method work?

▶ **Review Perimeter and Area**

Perimeter and Area

Perimeter and area are measured with different kinds of units: units of distance or length for perimeter and square units for area.

Perimeter is the total distance around the outside of a figure.

This rectangle has 4 units along its length and 3 units along its width. To find the perimeter, you add the distances of all of the sides:

$$l + w + l + w = P$$

Area is the total number of square units inside a figure.

For rectangles, area can be seen as an array of squares. This rectangle is an array of 4 squares across (length) and 3 squares down (width). To find its area, you can multiply length times width:

$$l \times w = A$$

▶ **Adapt the Formulas**

How can you change the equations for the area and perimeter of rectangles to apply to squares?

▶ Practice with Perimeter and Area

For each pair of rectangles, tell which one shows units of perimeter and find the perimeter. Tell which one shows units of area and find the area. Use 1 inch as the unit of length in all of your answers.

14.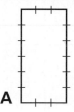

15.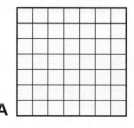

16.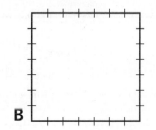

17.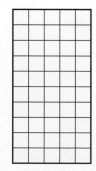

 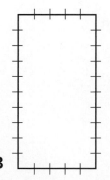

Show your work on your paper or in your Activity Workbook.

► Calculate Perimeter and Area

On one figure, draw in the units of area and find the area. On the other, draw in the units of perimeter and find the perimeter.

18.

9 mi

2 mi

2 mi

9 mi

$P =$ ☐

$A =$ ☐

19.

4 m

4 m

4 m

4 m

$P =$ ☐

$A =$ ☐

20.

6 cm

7 cm

7 cm

6 cm

$P =$ ☐

$A =$ ☐

21.

3 ft

5 ft

5 ft

3 ft

$P =$ ☐

$A =$ ☐

22. Challenge For one of the rectangles above, draw and label a different rectangle that has either the same area or the same perimeter.

▶ Compare Perimeter and Area

Copy and complete each table.

23. On centimeter-grid paper, draw every possible rectangle that has an area of 20 square centimeters and sides whose lengths are whole centimeters. Label the lengths of two adjacent sides of each rectangle.

24. Find and label the perimeter of each rectangle. Then complete the table.

25. Rectangles that have the same _____ ▪ can have different _____ ▪.

| Rectangles with an Area of 20 sq cm ||
Lengths in cm of Two Adjacent Sides	Perimeter
▪	▪
▪	▪
▪	▪

26. On centimeter-grid paper, draw every possible rectangle that has a perimeter of 18 centimeters and sides whose lengths are whole centimeters. Label the lengths of two adjacent sides of each rectangle.

27. Find and label the area of each rectangle. Then complete the table at the right.

28. Rectangles that have the same _____ ▪ can have different _____ ▪.

| Rectangles with a Perimeter of 18 cm ||
Lengths in cm of Two Adjacent Sides	Area
▪	▪
▪	▪
▪	▪
▪	▪

▶ Guess and Check

Use the Guess and Check strategy if there is no clear way to solve a problem. You can use a table to organize your guesses and checks.

Guess		Check	
Sara	Tim	Total	Is it 24?
8	8 × 3 = 24	8 + 24 = 32	No
7	7 × 3 = 21	7 + 21 = 28	No
6	6 × 3 = 18	6 + 18 = 24	Yes!

Tim bought three times as many books as Sara. Together, they bought 24 books. How many books did they each buy?

Step 1 Guess a number of books for Sara.

Step 2 Multiply that guess by 3 to get Tim's number of books.

Step 3 Add the two guesses to check if they total 24 books.

Answer: Sara bought 6 books and Tim bought 18 books.

Use the Guess and Check strategy to solve each problem.

1. Antwan is twice as old as Maria. The sum of their ages is 18 years. How old is Antwan? How old is Maria?

2. A rectangular patio has a perimeter of 36 yards. It is twice as long as it is wide. What are the length and width of the patio?

3. Wendy bought a new square tablecloth for her kitchen table. The area of the tablecloth is 25 square feet. What is the length of each side of the tablecloth?

4. There are 45 students in the math club. There are four times as many girls as boys in the club. How many boys are in the club? How many girls?

5. **Math Journal** Write a problem that can be solved with the Guess and Check strategy.

Class Activity

▶ Perimeter of a Parallelogram

In this **parallelogram**, b is the length of the **base** and s is the **slant height**. Here are three different ways to find the perimeter of the parallelogram.

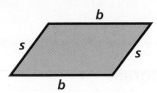

A Add the sides.

$$b + s + b + s = P$$

B Add the length of the base and the length of the slant height. Multiply the total by 2.

$$(b + s) \cdot 2 = P$$

C Multiply the length of the base by 2. Multiply the length of the slant height by 2. Find the total.

$$(b \cdot 2) + (s \cdot 2) = P$$

Answer questions 1–4 on a separate sheet of paper.

1. Why do the equations for rectangles also work for parallelograms?

2. Will equation **A** work for all quadrilaterals? Why or why not?

3. Will equations **B** and **C** work for quadrilaterals that are not parallelograms? Why or why not?

4. How can you change the equations to make them work for a **rhombus**?

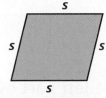

Class Activity

▶ **Parallelograms and Rectangles**

Vocabulary

perpendicular
base
height

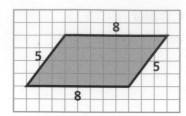

On a sheet of grid paper, draw a parallelogram exactly like the one above. Label the sides with their measurements.

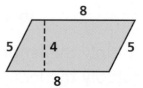

Draw a line segment inside that is **perpendicular** to the **base**.

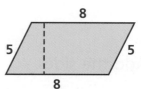

Measure the perpendicular line segment. It is called the **height**.

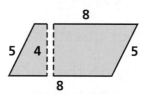

Cut the figure into two pieces along the height.

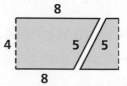

Move the left part over to the right so that the slanting sides touch.

5. What figure did you make?

Perimeter and Area of Parallelograms

▶ Parallelograms and Rectangles (continued)

Use your parallelogram to answer the questions.

6. What is the length of the rectangle?

7. What is the width?

8. Why can you use the formula for the area of a rectangle to find the area of the parallelogram?

9. Which measurement for the parallelogram do you not use to find the area? Why?

10. What is the area of the rectangle?

11. The bottom of a parallelogram is its base (*b*). The height (*h*) is perpendicular to the base. What formula can you write for the area of a parallelogram?

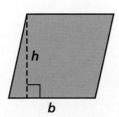

12. Why does this formula work for both rectangles and parallelograms?

Going Further

▶ **Change Rectangle Dimensions**

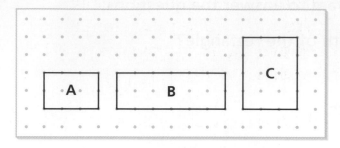

1. Rectangle B is twice as long as Rectangle A. How do their areas compare?

2. Rectangle C is twice as wide as Rectangle A. How do their areas compare?

3. What happens to the area when you double one side of the rectangle?

4. Draw a rectangle with sides that are double those of Rectangle D.

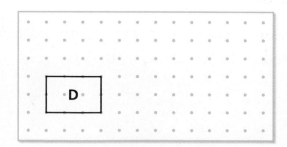

5. What happens to the area when you double both sides of a rectangle?

Perimeter and Area of Parallelograms

Class Activity

► Explore Complex Figures

City Park has a deep swimming pool for older children. This
year the city is planning to add a wading pool for younger
children next to the deep pool. In these drawings, the side
of each square unit represents 1 yard.

The deep pool:

The new pool:

Adding the wading pool:

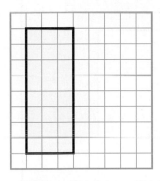
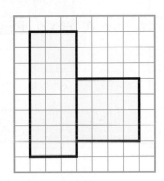
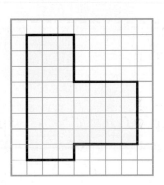

1. What is the shape of the deep pool?

2. What are its **perimeter** and **area**?

3. What is the shape of the wading pool?

4. What are its perimeter and area?

5. What is the area of the new pool?

6. What is the perimeter of the new pool?

7. Why is the area of the new pool the same as the area of the
   deep pool plus the area of the wading pool?

8. Why is the perimeter of the new pool not the same as the
   perimeter of the deep pool plus the perimeter of the wading pool?

▶ Perimeter and Area of Complex Figures

Find the perimeter and area of each figure.

9.

10.

11.

Perimeter and Area of Complex Figures

▶ Perimeter and Area of Complex Figures (continued)

Find the perimeter of each figure. Then divide each figure into rectangles and find the area. In these drawings, the side of each square unit represents 1 yard.

12.

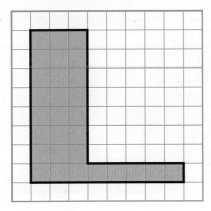

Perimeter: ▓

Area: ▓

13.

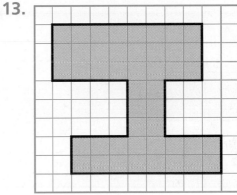

Perimeter: ▓

Area: ▓

14.

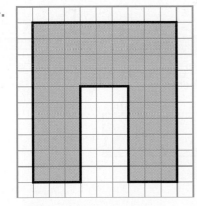

Perimeter: ▓

Area: ▓

15.

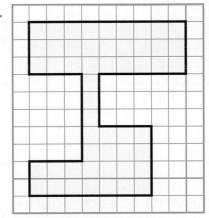

Perimeter: ▓

Area: ▓

16. **Explain Your Thinking** Why did you divide figure 12 the way you did?

Show your work on your paper or in your Activity Workbook.

▶ Find the Missing Dimensions

17. Some of the sides in figures A, B, C, and D are not labeled. Write the missing **dimensions**.

A

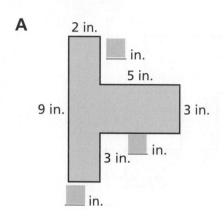

2 in.
___ in.
5 in.
9 in.
3 in.
3 in. ___ in.
___ in.

B

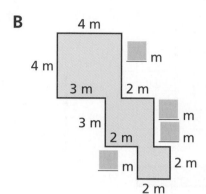

4 m
4 m ___ m
4 m
3 m 2 m
3 m
2 m ___ m
___ m
___ m
2 m
___ m
2 m

C

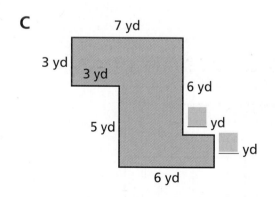

7 yd
3 yd
3 yd
6 yd
5 yd ___ yd
___ yd
6 yd

D

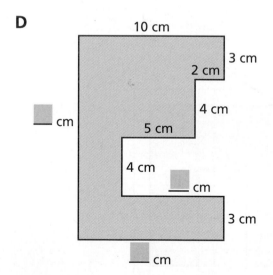

10 cm
3 cm
2 cm
4 cm
___ cm
5 cm
4 cm
___ cm
3 cm
___ cm

18. What is the area of each figure?

A: ▢   B: ▢   C: ▢   D: ▢

19. What is the perimeter of each figure?

A: ▢   B: ▢   C: ▢   D: ▢

Show your answers on your paper or in your Activity Workbook.

1. Draw a figure that is congruent to the one shown.

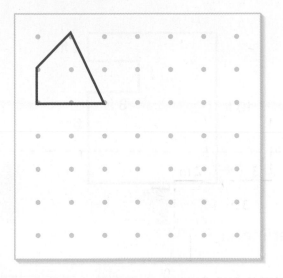

2. Draw all the lines of symmetry for the figure.

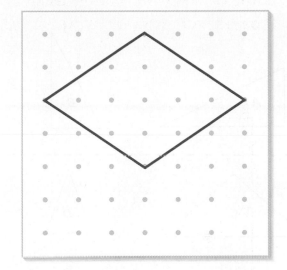

Describe each figure.

3.

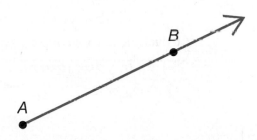

4.

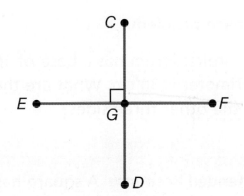

5.

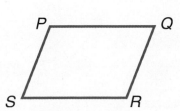

6.

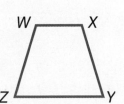

Name two shapes that appear to be similar.

7.

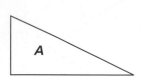

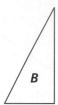

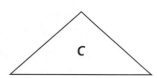

Find the perimeter and area of each figure. Show your work.

8.

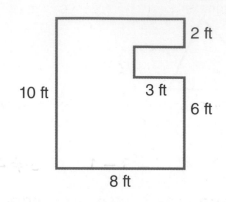

Perimeter

Area

Solve each problem.

9. A parallelogram has a base of 10 cm. Its perimeter is 30 cm. What are the lengths of the other three sides?

Show your work on your paper or in your journal.

10. **Extended Response** A square has an area of 25 sq ft. What is the length of one side? Sketch a picture and explain your reasoning.

Vocabulary

equation
sum
difference

▶ Discuss the = and ≠ Signs

An **equation** is made of two equal quantities or expressions. An equals sign (=) is used to show that the two sides are equal.

$5 = 3 + 2$ $3 + 2 = 5$ $5 = 5$ $3 + 2 = 2 + 3$ $7 - 2 = 1 + 1 + 3$

The "is not equal to" sign (≠) shows that two quantities are not equal.

$4 \neq 3 + 2$ $5 \neq 3 - 1$ $5 \neq 4$ $3 - 2 \neq 1 + 3$ $3 + 2 \neq 1 + 1 + 2$

An equation can have one or more numbers or letters on each side. A **sum** or **difference** can be written on either side of the equals sign.

1. Use the = sign to write four equations. Vary how many numbers you have on each side of your equations.

2. Use the ≠ sign to write four "is not equal to" statements. Vary how many numbers you have on each side of your ≠ signs.

Write = or ≠ to make each statement true.

3. $5 + 2 + 6$ ⬤ $6 + 7$ 4. 80 ⬤ $60 - 20$ 5. 70 ⬤ $40 + 30$

Vocabulary

Commutative Property of Addition

► Discuss the Commutative Property

The **Commutative Property of Addition** states that addition can be done in either order.

6. Does $3 + 2 = 2 + 3$?
   Tell why or why not.

7. Does $a + b = b + a$ for any two whole numbers?
   Tell why or why not.

8. Does the Commutative Property work for subtraction?
   Is $3 - 2 = 2 - 3$ a true statement?
   Tell why or why not.

Class Activity

▶ Discuss Inverse Operations

In addition you put two groups together. In subtraction you find an unknown addend or take away one group. Addition and subtraction are **inverse operations**. They undo each other.

Addends are numbers that are added to make a sum. You can find two addends of a number by breaking apart the number.

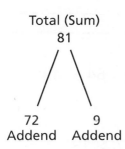

Total (Sum)
Addend
Addend

A break-apart drawing can help you find all eight related addition and subtraction equations for two addends.

Total (Sum)
81
72   9
Addend   Addend

$81 = 72 + 9$ $72 + 9 = 81$

$81 = 9 + 72$ $9 + 72 = 81$

$72 = 81 - 9$ $81 - 9 = 72$

$9 = 81 - 72$ $81 - 72 = 9$

9. Which equations show the Commutative Property?

10. What is the total in each equation. Where is the total in a subtraction equation?

Solve each equation.

11. $50 = 30 + p$

$p = \blacksquare$

12. $q + 20 = 60$

$q = \blacksquare$

13. $90 - v = 50$

$v = \blacksquare$

14. Write the eight related addition and subtraction equations for the break-apart drawing.

56
48   8

Going Further

Vocabulary

inequality

▶ Inequalities

A number sentence that shows that two amounts are not equal is an **inequality**. The "greater than" sign (>) shows that the quantity on the left is greater than the quantity on the right.

$$9 > 3 \qquad 6 > 0 \qquad 2 + 8 > 7$$

The "less than" sign (<) shows that the quantity on the left is less than the quantity on the right.

$$5 < 7 \qquad 0 < 1 \qquad 8 - 4 < 6$$

Write > or < to make each statement true.

1. 16 ⬤ 18

2. 55 ⬤ 47

3. 5 + 2 ⬤ 9

4. 25 + 15 ⬤ 35

5. 9 + 2 ⬤ 3 + 4 + 1

6. 120 ⬤ 84 + 44

Write + or − to make each statement true.

7. 5 ⬤ 2 < 6

8. 12 > 9 ⬤ 4

9. 8 ⬤ 7 > 13

10. 11 ⬤ 6 > 8

11. 22 ⬤ 9 < 19

12. 7 + 3 < 6 ⬤ 5

Write four numbers. Then write three different inequalities, using all four numbers in each inequality.

Understand Equality

Family Letter

Dear Family,

Your child is familiar with addition and subtraction problems from past years. Unit 3 of *Math Expressions* guides students as they deepen and extend their mastery of these operations. The main goals of this unit are:

- to help students gain speed and accuracy in addition and subtraction,
- to introduce algebraic expressions and equations that feature these operations,
- to help students see how addition and subtraction relate to real-world situations, and
- to begin exploring two-step problems and mixed word problems.

Your child will learn and practice techniques such as counting on, doubling, regrouping, and ungrouping to gain speed and accuracy in addition and subtraction. Parentheses, which will be used throughout the school year, will be introduced to show which operation should be done first. The symbols "=" and "≠" will be used to show whether numbers and expressions are equal.

Increasing and decreasing change problems will be introduced in which the starting number, the change, or the result will be unknown. Your child will learn how to write an equation to show a change, collection, or comparison situation, and then solve the equation to find the answer to that problem.

Finally, your child will apply this knowledge to solve word problems for which he or she will have to determine the operations needed to solve the problems and carry out a strategy to arrive at a solution.

If you have questions or comments, please contact your child's teacher.

Sincerely,
Your child's teacher

Your teacher will give you a a copy of this letter.

Carta a la familia

Estimada familia:

Durante los últimos años, su niño se ha familiarizado con problemas de suma y de resta. La Unidad 3 de *Math Expressions* guía a los estudiantes a medida que refuerzan y amplían su habilidad con estas operaciones. Los objetivos principales de esta unidad son:

- ayudar a los estudiantes a adquirir rapidez y exactitud con la suma y la resta,
- presentar expresiones algebraicas y ecuaciones que requieren estas operaciones,
- ayudar a los estudiantes a ver de qué manera la suma y la resta se relacionan con situaciones de la vida real y
- empezar a practicar problemas de dos pasos y problemas verbales mixtos.

Su niño aprenderá y practicará técnicas como contar hacia adelante, duplicar, reagrupar y desagrupar para adquirir rapidez y exactitud con la suma y la resta. A lo largo del año escolar se presentarán los paréntesis, los cuales se usarán para mostrar qué operaciones se deben hacer primero. Los símbolos $=$ y $\neq$ se usarán para mostrar si los números y expresiones son iguales.

Se presentarán problemas con cambios de aumento o de disminución en los cuales el número inicial, el cambio o el resultado serán desconocidos. Su niño aprenderá a escribir una ecuación para mostrar una situación relacionada con cambio, colección o comparación, y luego a resolver la ecuación y así hallar la respuesta al problema.

Por último, su niño aplicará este conocimiento para resolver problemas verbales, para los que deberá determinar las operaciones necesarias para resolverlos y usar una estrategia para hallar una solución.

Si tiene alguna pregunta o comentario, por favor comuníquese conmigo.

Atentamente,
El maestro de su niño

Tu maestro te dará una copia de esta carta.

Understand Equality

3–2

Class Activity

Vocabulary

situation equation
solution equation

▶ Discuss Change Problems

Change Situations	
Change Plus:	Start + Change = Result
Change Minus:	Start − Change = Result

Read each problem and discuss the equations.

A. At the park, 6 children were playing. Some more children came to the park. Now, 13 children are at the park. How many more children came to the park?
Situation Equation: $6 + c = 13$
Solution Equation: $13 - 6 = c$

B. At the park, some children were playing. Then 20 children had to go home. Now 30 children are left. How many children were at the park first?
Situation Equation: $p - 20 = 30$
Solution Equation: $20 + 30 = p$

▶ Solve Change Problems

Write a situation equation or a solution equation, using a letter to represent the unknown. Make a math drawing if you need to.

Show your work on your paper or in your journal.

1. One afternoon, 63 books were checked out of a library. That day, 72 books in all were checked out. How many books were checked out that morning?

2. At noon, 70 students went to the school cafeteria for lunch. After 15 minutes, only 19 of those students remained. How many students left the cafeteria during that time?

Class Activity

Vocabulary
change plus
change minus

▶ Write Change Problems

Choose 2 equations. Write a **change plus** or a **change minus** word problem to represent each situation equation.

$$35 + n = 40 \qquad n - 20 = 5 \qquad 5 + 40 = n$$

$$n + 40 = 45 \qquad 45 - n = 20 \qquad 50 - 5 = n$$

3. Change plus

> Show your work on your paper or in your journal.

4. Change minus

> Show your work on your paper or in your journal.

Vocabulary

collection situations

▶ Discuss Collection Problems

Collection situations involve a total amount broken into two addends. There are three kinds of collection situations.

No Action: The problem describes the total and the addends.

Put Together: The two addends are put together to make the total.

Take Apart: The total is taken apart to make the two addends.

Collection situations can have an unknown total or an unknown addend (partner). You can use a break-apart drawing to relate the addends and the total. Or you can write a situation or solution equation.

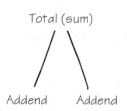

Total (sum)

Addend   Addend

1. Elizabeth's mother picked 9 blue flowers and 7 red flowers. How many flowers did Elizabeth's mother pick?

2. A fruit bowl contains 18 pieces of fruit. Of these, 13 are apples and the rest are bananas. How many bananas are in the bowl?

Break-Apart Drawings

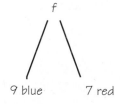

f

9 blue   7 red

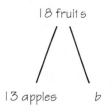

18 fruits

13 apples b

Situation Equations: $f = 9 + 7$ $18 = 13 + b$

Solution Equations: $9 + 7 = f$ $18 - 13 = b$ or $13 + b = 18$

Class Activity

▶ Solve Collection Problems

Make a break-apart drawing for each problem. Then write and solve an equation using a letter to represent the unknown.

Show your work on your paper or in your journal.

3. A stamp collection contains 90 domestic stamps and 40 foreign stamps. How many stamps does the collection contain altogether?

4. The enrollment in a small middle school is 130 students. Of those students, 70 are girls. How many students in the school are boys?

5. A school has 110 folding chairs. Some chairs are in storage and the other 80 chairs are in the auditorium. How many chairs are in storage?

6. Noreen put $10 in her pocket and the other $35 in her wallet. How much money does Noreen have?

7. The 1:00 P.M. showing of a movie had 50 adults and 60 children in the audience. How many people attended the movie?

8. In a collection of 200 coins, 20 coins are pennies. How many coins in the collection are not pennies?

Addition and Subtraction Collection Problems

► Write the Appropriate Label

Write a label to complete each answer.

9. 9 adults + 5 children = 14

10. 7 dimes + 1 penny = 8

11. 8 apples + 8 oranges = 16

12. 4 cats + 6 dogs = 10

► Break-Apart Drawings

Write a collection problem for each break-apart drawing.
Then solve the problems.

13.
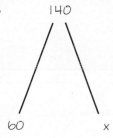

14.
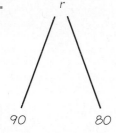

15. **On the Back** Make a break-apart drawing. Then write and solve a problem, using your drawing.

Addition and Subtraction Collection Problems

Class Activity

▶ Discuss Comparison Situations

In Unit 1, you learned about multiplication and division **comparison situations**. You can also compare by addition and subtraction. You can find *how much more* or *how much less* one amount is than another.

The amount more or less is called the **difference**. In some problems, the difference is not given. You have to find it. In other problems, the smaller or the larger amount is not given.

Mai has 9 apples and 12 plums.

- How many more plums than apples does she have?

- How many fewer apples than plums does she have?

Plums | 12

Apples | 9 | d

Comparison bars can help us show which is more. We show the difference in an oval.

Draw comparison bars for each problem. Write and solve an equation. Discuss other equations you could use.

1. The nursery has 70 rose bushes and 50 tea-tree bushes. How many fewer tea-tree bushes than rose bushes are at the nursery?

2. Dan wants to plant 30 trees. He has dug 21 holes. How many trees don't have a hole yet?

▶ Discuss the Language

The large amount or the small amount can be the unknown. Some comparing sentences have **leading** language that suggests what to do. Other comparing sentences have **misleading** language that may trick you into doing the wrong operation.

Copy and label the comparison bars and solve. Say the reverse comparing sentence to see if it helps you.

3. There are 10 dogs at the kennel. There are 6 fewer dogs than cats. How many cats are at the kennel?

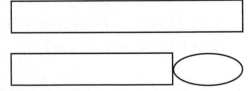

4. There are 15 girls in Ms. Roedel's fourth-grade class. There are 3 more girls than boys. How many boys are there?

Addition and Subtraction Comparison Problems

▶ Share Solutions

Draw comparison bars for each problem. Write and solve an equation. Don't let misleading language trick you!

5. At the zoo there are 7 monkeys. There are 6 more kangaroos than monkeys. How many kangaroos are at the zoo?

6. The soccer team drilled for 50 minutes. It drilled 10 minutes longer than it scrimmaged. How long did the soccer team scrimmage?

7. Avery is 13 years old. He is 4 years older than Marisa. How old is Marisa?

8. Sabrina studied 15 more minutes than Sean. How long did Sean study if Sabrina studied for 45 minutes?

9. On the last day of school, 10 more students wore shorts than wore jeans. If 13 students wore jeans, how many students wore shorts?

10. **On the Back** Write a comparison problem. Show comparison bars and an equation to solve your problem.

Write your answer to the "On the Back" question on your paper or in your journal.

Addition and Subtraction Comparison Problems

▶ Discuss the Steps of the Problem

Sometimes you will need to work through more than one step to solve a problem. The steps can be shown in one or more equations.

1. In the morning, 19 students were working on a science project. In the afternoon, 3 students left and 7 more students came to work on the project. How many students were working on the project at the end of the day?

2. Solve the problem again by finishing Tommy's and Lucy's methods. Then discuss what is alike and what is different about each method.

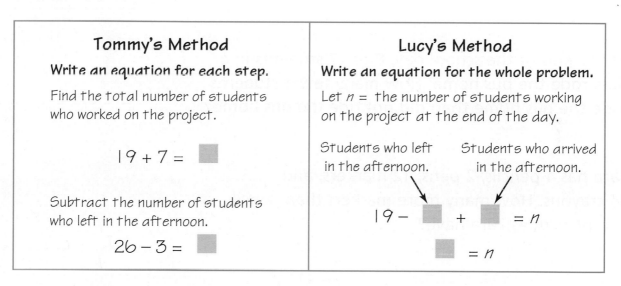

Tommy's Method

Write an equation for each step.

Find the total number of students who worked on the project.

$19 + 7 = \blacksquare$

Subtract the number of students who left in the afternoon.

$26 - 3 = \blacksquare$

Lucy's Method

Write an equation for the whole problem.

Let $n =$ the number of students working on the project at the end of the day.

Students who left in the afternoon.   Students who arrived in the afternoon.

$19 - \blacksquare + \blacksquare = n$

$\blacksquare = n$

3. Solve. Discuss the steps you used.

A team is scheduled to play 12 games. Of those games, 7 will be played at home. The other games are away games. How many fewer away games than home games will be played?

▶ Share Solutions

Solve each problem mentally or use equations, comparison bars, or break-apart drawings.

Show your work on your paper or in your journal.

4. A garden contains 54 vegetable plants. Altogether, the garden has 63 fruit and vegetable plants. How many fewer fruit plants than vegetable plants are there?

5. Tyler is thinking of a number. If 5 is added to his number and 8 is subtracted from the total, the result is 2. What is Tyler's number?

6. At the end of the school day, 8 of 17 students in a class rode the bus home. How many fewer students rode the bus home than did not ride the bus home?

7. Zara has 4 pencils, 2 pens, 12 markers, and 24 crayons. How many more markers than pencils and pens does Zara have?

8. Hannah studied for 40 minutes on the evening before a test. On the day of the test, she studied for 15 minutes before school and for 10 minutes after lunch. Did Hannah study for more than one hour? Explain your answer.

Two-Step Problems Using Addition and Subtraction

Class Activity

▶ Discuss Types of Problems

Addition and Subtraction Situations

Addition and subtraction problems involve two **addends** and a **total**. Either the total or one addend will be unknown.

1. Hassan had 5 marbles. Jenny gave him more marbles. Now Hassan has 14 marbles. How many marbles did Jenny give Hassan?

2. After spending 40¢, Michael has 6 dimes. How much money did he start with?

3. Eliza has $15. This amount is $7 less than she had yesterday. How much money did Eliza have yesterday?

4. The school has 20 windows open. There are 50 windows altogether. How many windows are closed?

Multiplication and Division Situations

Multiplication and division involve repeated groups of the same size.

5. Jevon has 30 trading cards. He has 3 times as many as Ramon. How many trading cards does Ramon have?

6. Jenita had 5 baskets of apples with 10 apples in each basket. She gave away 2 baskets. How many apples does she have now?

Do you need to multiply or divide to solve this problem?

What operations do you need to do to solve this problem?

▶ Share Solutions

Solve.

Show your work on your paper or in your journal.

7. A math test was given to 26 students. After 20 minutes, 9 students had completed the test. What number of students took more than 20 minutes to complete the test?

8. Anna spent $18 for a pair of jeans and had $32 left over. How much money did Anna have before she bought the jeans?

9. A class has 24 students. The teacher wants to make 3 math teams with the same number of students on each team. How many students will be on each team?

10. Jason receives five dollars each week for his allowance. His older brother gets 3 times as much as Jason. How much does Jason's older brother get after two weeks?

11. The faculty of a school is made up of 17 female teachers. There are 2 more female teachers than male teachers. How many teachers are at the school altogether?

12. A box contains 60 oranges. A basket contains $\frac{1}{3}$ as many apples as oranges. How many apples are in the basket?

Mixed Word Problems

Class Activity

Vocabulary
place-value drawings
dot array

▶ Represent Hundreds

You can represent numbers by making **place-value drawings** on a **dot array**.

1. What number does this drawing show?
   Explain your thinking.

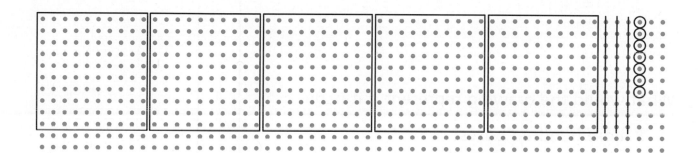

▶ Represent Thousands

Discuss this place-value drawing. Write the number of each.

2. ones: ⬚

3. quick tens: ⬚

4. hundred boxes: ⬚

5. thousand bars: ⬚

6. How many hundred boxes could we draw inside each thousand bar? Explain.

7. What number does this drawing show?

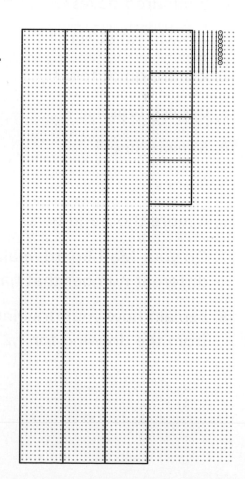

▶ Draw Larger Numbers

Place value can also be shown without using a dot array.

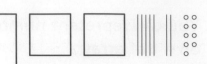

8. What number does this drawing represent?
Explain your thinking.

What would the drawing represent if it had:

9. 3 more hundred boxes?

10. 0 hundred boxes?

11. 2 fewer quick tens?

12. 2 more quick tens?

13. 0 quick tens?

14. 5 fewer ones?

15. 0 ones?

16. 4 more thousand bars?

17. On your MathBoard, make a place-value drawing for a different number that has the digits 1, 2, 7, and 9.

18. Explain how your drawing is similar to and different from the drawing for 1,279.

▶ Practice With Place-Value Drawings

Make a place-value drawing for each number, using ones, quick tens, hundred boxes, and thousand bars.

19. 6

20. 3

21. 603

22. 300

23. 63

24. 32

25. 325

26. 3,285

27. 109

28. 573

Going Further

▶ Place Value and Money

Mr. Jansen wants to buy a television for $214. He doesn't have 214 dollar bills in his pocket! What bills can Mr. Jansen use to pay for the television?

We can use place value to see how Mr. Jansen can pay for the television.

$214 = 200 + 10 + 4$

$\$214 = \$200 + \$10 + \$4$

Mr. Jansen can use 2 hundred-dollar bills, 1 ten-dollar bill, and 4 one-dollar bills to pay for the television.

Write the amount shown.

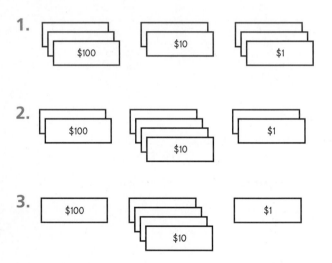

1.

2.

3.

4. Ron deposited 7 hundred-dollar bills and 6 one-dollar bills into his bank account. Write the amount he deposited.

5. Fran has 3 hundred-dollar bills, 8 ten-dollar bills, and 20 one-dollar bills. What is the fewest number of bills she could receive in exchange?

Dear Family,

Beginning today, your child will be learning about place values in our number system and about how to read and write large numbers. In a few days, your child will learn about addition with large numbers. An important concept is that we need to add digits with the same place value. We must add ones to ones, tens to tens, and so on. The *Math Expressions* program encourages children to think about "making new groups" to help them understand place values.

We call the addition method below "New Groups Above" because the numbers that represent the new groups are written above the problem.

1. Add the ones:
5 + 7 = 12 ones
12 = 2 ones + 10 ones, and 10 ones = 1 new ten.

2. Add the tens:
1 + 7 + 6 = 14 tens
14 = 4 tens + 10 tens, and 10 tens = 1 new hundred.

3. Add the hundreds:
1 + 1 = 2 hundreds

Step 2 is harder because you need to add the 1 to 7 and remember 8 and then add 8 and 6.

```
 (1)         (1)1        1 1
 175         175        1 1 75
+ 67        + 67       +  67
---          ---        ------
  2          42         2 4 2
```

We call the following method "New Groups Below." The steps are the same as those above, but the new groups are written below the addends.

It is easier to see the totals for each column (12 and 14) and adding is easier because you add the two numbers you see and then add the 1 (7 + 6 + 1).

```
1.    175      2.    175      3.    175
     + 67           + 67           + 67
     -----          -----          -----
       2             42             242
```

It is important that your child maintain his or her home practice with basic multiplication and division. If you need practice items or materials, please contact me.

Sincerely,
Your child's teacher

Your teacher will give you a a copy of this letter.

Carta a la familia

Estimada familia:

A partir de hoy, su niño aprenderá los valores posicionales de nuestro sistema numérico, y a leer y escribir números grandes. Dentro de unos días, su niño aprenderá a sumar números grandes. Un concepto importante es que debemos sumar dígitos del mismo valor posicional. Debemos sumar unidades con unidades, decenas con decenas, y así sucesivamente. El programa *Math Expressions* anima a los niños a pensar en "hacer grupos nuevos" para ayudarlos a comprender los valores posicionales.

El método de suma que se muestra se llama "Grupos nuevos arriba" porque los números que representan los grupos nuevos se escriben arriba del problema.

1. Suma las unidades:
5 + 7 = 12 unidades
12 = 2 unidades
+ 10 unidades,
y 10 unidades =
1 nueva decena.

2. Suma las decenas:
1 + 7 + 6 = 14 decenas
14 = 4 decenas
+ 10 decenas,
y 10 decenas =
1 nueva centena.

3. Suma las centenas:
1 + 1 = 2 centenas

El paso 2 es más difícil porque hay que sumar el 1 al 7, recordar el 8 y luego sumar 8 + 6.

```
  (1)            (1)(1)           1 1
 175            1 75            1 175
+ 67           + 67           +  67
────           ────           ─────
   2             42            1 242
```

Al siguiente método le damos el nombre de "Grupos nuevos abajo".

Es más fácil ver los totales de cada columna (12 y 14) y sumar porque sumas los dos números que ves, y luego sumas 1 (7 + 6 + 1).

1.
```
 175
+ 67
────
  (2)
```

2.
```
 175
+ 67
────
 (4)2
```

3.
```
 175
+ 67
────
 242
```

Es importante que su niño siga practicando las multiplicaciones y divisiones básicas en casa. Si usted necesita elementos o materiales para practicar, por favor comuníquese conmigo.

Atentamente,
El maestro de su niño

Tu maestro te dará una copia de esta carta.

Place Value to Thousands

► Write Numbers Different Ways

Standard form: 8,562
Word form: eight thousand, five hundred sixty-two
Expanded form: 8,000 + 500 + 60 + 2
Place value form: 8 thousands 5 hundreds 6 tens 2 ones

Write each number in expanded form.

1. 73

2. 108

3. 621

4. 4,350

5. 8,083

6. 1,006

Write each number in standard form.

7. 40 + 3

8. 200 + 60 + 1

9. 900 + 5

10. 1,000 + 70 + 9

11. 5,000 + 30

12. 9,000 + 800 + 4

Write each number in word form.

13. 400 + 40 + 1

14. 1,000 + 50

Write each number in standard form and in place value form.

15. thirty-five

16. three hundred five

17. three hundred fifty

18. three hundred fifteen

19. six thousand, eight

20. six thousand, one hundred eight

Write the value of the underlined digit.

21. 7<u>5</u>6

22. <u>4</u>,851

23. 6,<u>5</u>07

► Other Representations

Any number can be represented in many different ways.

$100 = 90 + 6 + 4$ $100 = 110 - 10$ $100 = 10 \times 10$ $100 = 200 \div 2$

Represent each number a different way.

24. 1,200

25. 3,456

26. 675

27. 287

28. 149

29. 500

30. 1,000

31. 9,001

► Discuss Rounding Numbers

Round to the nearest ten. Make a rounding frame for the first number.

32. 87

33. 16

34. 71

35. 65

36. 14

37. 98

Round to the nearest hundred. Make a rounding frame for the first number.

38. 734

39. 363

40. 178

41. 249

42. 251

43. 992

Round to the nearest thousand. Make a rounding frame for the first number.

44. 1,275

45. 8,655

46. 5,482

47. 3,804

48. 1,501

49. 9,702

Class Activity

Vocabulary

greater than >
less than <
digit

▶ Compare Numbers

Discuss the problem below.

Jim has 24 trading cards and Hattie has 42 trading cards.
Who has more trading cards? How do you know?

Write **>** (greater than), **<** (less than), or **=** to make each
statement true.

1. 26 ⬤ 29   2. 44 ⬤ 34   3. 26 ⬤ 62

4. 74 ⬤ 77   5. 85 ⬤ 58   6. 126 ⬤ 162

7. 253 ⬤ 235   8. 620 ⬤ 602   9. 825 ⬤ 528

10. 478 ⬤ 488   11. 3,294 ⬤ 3,924   12. 8,925 ⬤ 9,825

13. 6,706 ⬤ 6,760   14. 4,106 ⬤ 4,016   15. 1,997 ⬤ 1,799

▶ Greatest and Least

Write the *greatest* and the *least* four-digit number
possible. Use each of the 4 digits in the group exactly once.

16. 6, 3, 8, 2   17. 4, 9, 1, 5

    Greatest: ⬛   Greatest: ⬛

    Least: ⬛   Least: ⬛

18. 0, 6, 7, 3   19. 0, 4, 0, 1

    Greatest: ⬛   Greatest: ⬛

    Least: ⬛   Least: ⬛

▶ **Use a Number Line**

Show your work on your paper or in your Activity Workbook.

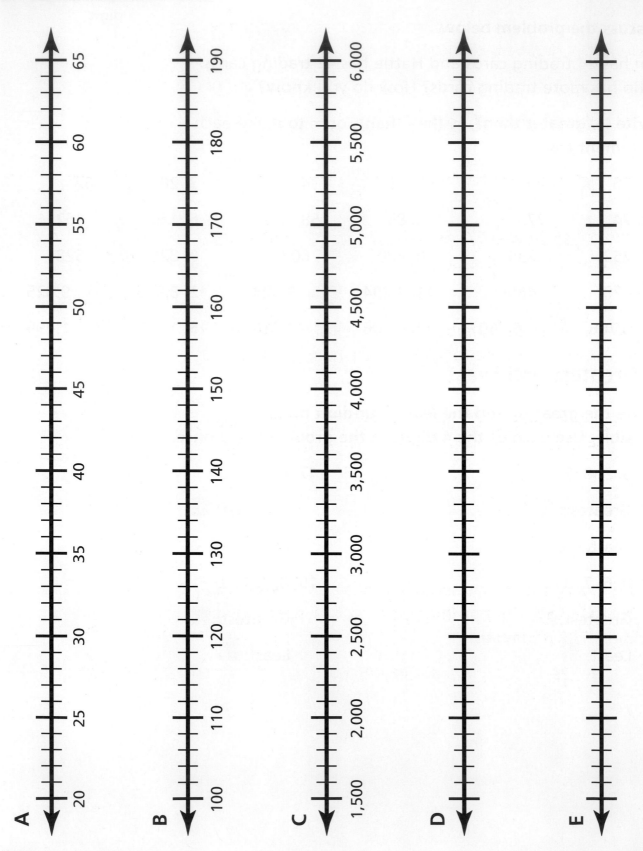

A
65
60
55
50
45
40
35
30
25
20

B
190
180
170
160
150
140
130
120
110
100

C
6,000
5,500
5,000
4,500
4,000
3,500
3,000
2,500
2,000
1,500

D

E

Compare Whole Numbers

Show your work on your paper or in your Activity Workbook.

► **Compare Numbers on a Number Line**

The range of numbers that fall between 25 and 55 does not include the numbers 25 and 55.

20. Circle the numbers 25 and 55 on the number line below.

21. Shade the range of numbers between 25 and 55.

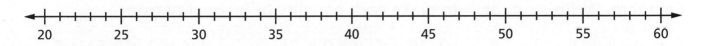

22. Put Xs on 27 and 57. Are both 27 and 57 within the range 25 to 55? Explain.

23. Think about the number range 110 to 190. Are both 117 and 171 within the range? Explain how you know.

24. Think about the number range 1,500 to 1,700. Are both 1,705 and 1,507 within the range? Explain how you know.

► **Ordering Numbers**

Write each group of numbers in order from greatest to least. Then tell whether the first or last number is closer to the middle number.

25. 20, 10, 29   **26.** 68, 75, 60   **27.** 120, 100, 200

Going Further

Vocabulary

equality
inequality

► Compare Expressions

An **equality** is an equation that indicates two amounts are equal, and includes an equals (=) sign. An **inequality** is a statement that indicates two amounts are not equal, and includes a greater than sign (>) or a less than sign (<).

$$8 - 4 = 12 \div 3 \qquad 9 + 5 > 2 \times 6 \qquad 10 \times 0 < 3 - 2$$

Compare. Write >, <, or = to make each equality or inequality true.

1. $6 \times 3 \bigcirc 6 + 3$
2. $16 - 5 \bigcirc 9 + 2$
3. $4 \times 2 \bigcirc 54 \div 6$

4. $14 \div 2 \bigcirc 8 - 1$
5. $4 \times 7 \bigcirc 2 \times 12$
6. $40 \div 8 \bigcirc 3 \times 2$

7. $19 - 18 \bigcirc 4 \times 4$
8. $6 \div 1 \bigcirc 6 \div 6$
9. $7 \times 0 \bigcirc 9 - 9$

Write numbers to make true statements.

10. $\blacksquare + \blacksquare < \blacksquare - \blacksquare$
11. $\blacksquare \div \blacksquare > \blacksquare \times \blacksquare$

12. $\blacksquare \times \blacksquare > \blacksquare \div \blacksquare$
13. $\blacksquare - \blacksquare < \blacksquare + \blacksquare$

► Properties

Use what you know about properties to make each statement true. Write the name of the property you used.

14. $b + a = \blacksquare + b$ _____

15. $\blacksquare \bullet z = z$ _____

16. $(r \bullet s) \bullet t = r \bullet (s \bullet \blacksquare)$ _____

17. $n = n + \blacksquare$ _____

18. $p \bullet y = \blacksquare \bullet p$ _____

19. $e + (\blacksquare + d) = (e + c) + d$ _____

Compare Whole Numbers

Vocabulary
place value

▶ Identify Place Value

To read and write numbers, you need to understand **place value**.

1. What are the names of the places of a 3-digit number?

Hundreds	Tens	Ones
2	3	5

2. How do we read and write 235 with words?

Hundred Thousands	Ten Thousands	Thousands	,	Hundreds	Tens	Ones
4	6	8	,	2	3	5

3. Read the number 8,235. Then write 8,235 using words.

4. Read the number 68,235. Then write 68,235 using words.

5. Read the number 468,235. Then write 468,235 using words.

Hundred Millions	Ten Millions	Millions	,	Hundred Thousands	Ten Thousands	Thousands	,	Hundreds	Tens	Ones
1	7	9	,	4	6	8	,	2	3	5

6. Read the number 9,468,235. Then write 9,468,235 using words.

7. Read the number 79,468,235. Then write it using words.

8. Read the number 179,468,235. Then write it using words.

▶ Read and Write Large Numbers

Read each number aloud.

9. 39,012   10. 5,709,812   11. 640,739,812   12. 358,917,426

13. 102,453,068   14. 460,053,105   15. 297,365,004   16. 862,050,139

Write each number in words.

17. 9,802

18. 730,812

19. 45,039,812

20. 521,600,439

Write each number in standard form.

21. two thousand, fifty-three

22. one hundred forty thousand, one hundred four

23. seventy-six thousand, five

24. three million, fifty-nine thousand, two hundred sixty-one

25. seven hundred thousand, four hundred thirty

26. four hundred eighty-six million, thirty-one thousand, two hundred seventy-nine

▶ Discuss Different Methods

Discuss how each part of the place-value drawing is related to each addition method.

879

+

754

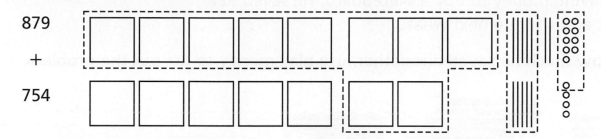

1. New Groups Above Method

Step 1	Step 2	Step 3
¹	¹¹	¹¹
879	879	879
+ 754	+ 754	+ 754
3	33	1,633

2. New Groups Below Method

Step 1	Step 2	Step 3
879	879	879
+ 754	+ 754	+ 754
3	33	1,633

3. Show Subtotals Method

Left-to-Right   Right-to-Left

Step 1	Step 2	Step 3	Step 4		Right-to-Left
879	879	879	879		879
+ 754	+ 754	+ 754	+ 754		+ 754
1,500	1,500	1,500	**1,500**		13
	120	120	120		120
		13	+ 13.		+ 1,500
			1,633		1,633

4. Discuss how each method above shows new groups.

5. On a separate sheet of paper, describe how the Left-to-Right solution and the Right-to-Left solution are alike and how they are different.

▶ Addition and Money

You can use models to help you add money amounts.

> *Show your work on your paper or in your journal.*

Carlos is saving money to buy a skateboard. He saved $27 one week and $14 the next week.

To find how much he saved altogether, use play money to act out the problem.

Use play money to solve each problem.

1. Robyn's grandmother gave her $38 for her birthday and her uncle gave her $25. How much did Robyn get altogether?

2. Melise's family bought a table for $264 and a chair for $172. How much did the family pay for the table and chair together?

3. A parent-teacher club sold baked goods to raise money for the school. They collected $268 on Friday and $479 on Saturday. How much did they collect altogether?

Make New Groups for Addition

▶ Analyze Different Methods

New Groups Above

Step 1
```
  ¹
  56,973,608
+  8,591,729
            7
```

Step 2
```
     ¹
  56,973,608
+  8,591,729
           37
```

Step 3
```
    ¹ ¹
  56,973,608
+  8,591,729
          337
```

Step 4
```
     ¹
  56,973,608
+  8,591,729
        5,337
```

Step 5
```
    ¹   ¹
  56,973,608
+  8,591,729
       65,337
```

Step 6
```
   ¹  ¹ ¹
  56,973,608
+  8,591,729
      565,337
```

Step 7
```
  ¹ ¹  ¹ ¹
  56,973,608
+  8,591,729
    5,565,337
```

Step 8
```
 ¹ ¹ ¹  ¹ ¹
  56,973,608
+  8,591,729
   65,565,337
```

New Groups Below

Step 1
```
  56,973,608
+  8,59₁1,729
            7
```

Step 2
```
  56,973,608
+  8,59₁1,729
           37
```

Step 3
```
  56,973,608
+  8,59₁1,729
          337
```

Step 4
```
  56,973,608
+  8,59₁1,729
        5,337
```

Step 5
```
  56,973,608
+  8,591,729
       65,337
```

Step 6
```
  56,973,608
+  8,591,729
      565,337
```

Step 7
```
  56,973,608
+  8,591,729
    5,565,337
```

Step 8
```
  56,973,608
+  8,591,729
   65,565,337
```

Show Subtotals (Left-to-Right)

Step 1
```
  56,973,608
+  8,591,729
  50,000,000
```

Step 2
```
  56,973,608
+  8,591,729
  50,000,000
  14,000,000
```

Step 3
```
  56,973,608
+  8,591,729
  50,000,000
  14,000,000
   1,400,000
```

Step 4
```
  56,973,608
+  8,591,729
  50,000,000
  14,000,000
   1,400,000
     160,000
```

Step 5
```
  55,973,608
+  3,591,729
  50,000,000
  14,000,000
   1,400,000
     160,000
       4,000
```

Step 6
```
  56,973,608
+  8,591,729
  50,000,000
  14,000,000
   1,400,000
     160,000
       4,000
       1,300
```

Steps 7 & 8
```
  56,973,608
+  8,591,729
  50,000,000
  14,000,000
   1,400,000
     160,000
       4,000
       1,300
          20
          17
```

Step 9
```
  56,973,608
+  8,591,729
  50,000,000
  14,000,000
   1,400,000
     160,000
       4,000
       1,300
          20
+         17
  65,565,337
```

Vocabulary

digit

▶ Find the Mistake

When you add, it is important that you add **digits** in like places.

Look at the these addition exercises.

43,629 + 5,807   1,468 + 327,509   8,570,952 + 4,306

$$\begin{array}{r} 43,629 \\ + 5,807 \\ \hline 101,699 \end{array}$$
$$\begin{array}{r} 1,468 \\ + 327,509 \\ \hline 474,309 \end{array}$$
$$\begin{array}{r} 8,570,952 \\ + 4,306 \\ \hline 9,001,552 \end{array}$$

1. What mistake appears in all three exercises above?

▶ Practice Aligning Places

Copy each exercise, lining up places correctly. Then add. Show your new groups.

2. 2,647 + 38 = ▉

3. 156 + 83,291 = ▉

4. 4,389 + 49,706 = ▉

5. 135,826 + 2,927 = ▉

6. 2,347,092 + 6,739 = ▉

7. 15,231 + 57,697,084 = ▉

8. Write an addition word problem that has an answer of $43,568.

▶ Use Estimating

You can use rounding to estimate a total. Then you can adjust your estimated total to find the exact total.

The best-selling fruits at Joy's Fruit Shack are peaches and bananas. During one month Joy sold 397 peaches and 412 bananas.

1. *About* how many peaches and bananas did she sell in all?

2. *Exactly* how many peaches and bananas did she sell?

Estimate. Then adjust your estimate to find the exact answer.

3. $89 + 28 =$ ▨

4. $153 + 98 =$ ▨

5. $1,297 + 802 =$ ▨

6. $1,066 + 45,104 =$ ▨

Solve.

Tomás has $20.00 for some toys. The 3 toys he wants cost $3.98, $4.95, and $2.85. He also wants to buy 2 action figures that are 2 for $7.50.

Show your work on your paper or in your journal.

7. How can Tomás figure out whether he has enough money for all five items? Does he have enough?

8. Explain how he can figure out how much change he should get.

▶ Use Estimating (continued)

Solve.

Show your work on your paper or in your journal.

Mack has $5.00 for school supplies. He needs to buy 2 notebooks for $0.98 each. He also needs to buy 10 pencils for $0.20 each and 2 pens for $0.48 each.

9. Does he have enough money? How do you know?

10. How much more or less than $5.00 do his school supplies cost?

▶ Look for "Easy" Combinations

You can sometimes find number combinations that make it possible to add numbers mentally.

11. Add 243, 274, 252, and 231 vertically.

12. Explain how you can use number combinations to help you add the numbers.

Find the total. Add mentally if you can.

13.	14.	15.	16.	17.
8	46	35	348	147
4	21	29	516	182
6	+64	75	+ 492	108
+ 2	■	+ 61	■	+ 165
■		■		■

Class Activity

▶ Understand a Take-Apart Situation

Jimmy dropped a 400-piece jigsaw puzzle and the pieces went all over his room. He found 264 of them. This is how he used his MathBoard to find out how many pieces were still missing.

Discuss each step of Jimmy's drawing.

1. Jimmy drew 400 and wrote the numbers for the problem.

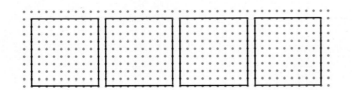

$$\begin{array}{r} 400 \\ -264 \\ \end{array}$$

2. Jimmy saw that he had no tens and no ones. What do his drawing and the numbers show that he did next?

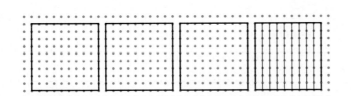

3. Then, what did he do to his drawing and numbers?

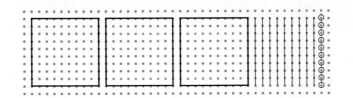

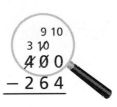

4. Next, he circled and drew a line through parts of the drawing. What does this show?

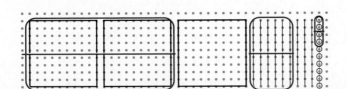

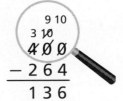

5. **On the Back** Explain how you ungroup 200 to subtract 25.

Subtract from Hundreds

Dear Family,

Your child is now learning about subtraction. A common subtraction mistake is subtracting in the wrong direction. Children may think that they always subtract the smaller digit from the larger digit, but this is not true. To help children avoid this mistake, the *Math Expressions* program encourages children to "fix" numbers first and then subtract.

$$\begin{array}{r} \cancel{634} \\ -\ \cancel{158} \\ \hline \cancel{524} \end{array}$$

When one or more digits in the top number are smaller than the corresponding digits in the bottom number, fix the numbers by "ungrouping." For example, 634 − 158 is shown below:

1. We cannot subtract 8 ones from 4 ones. We get more ones by ungrouping 1 ten to make 10 ones.

We now have 14 ones and only 2 tens.

$$\begin{array}{r} {\scriptstyle 2\ 14} \\ 6\,\cancel{3}\,\cancel{4} \\ -\ 1\,5\,8 \\ \hline \end{array}$$

2. We cannot subtract 5 tens from 2 tens. We get more tens by ungrouping 1 hundred to make 10 tens.

We now have 12 tens and only 5 hundreds.

$$\begin{array}{r} {\scriptstyle 12} \\ {\scriptstyle 5\ \cancel{2}\ 14} \\ \cancel{6}\,\cancel{3}\,\cancel{4} \\ -\ 1\,5\,8 \\ \hline \end{array}$$

3. Now we can subtract:
$5 - 1 = 4$ hundreds
$12 - 5 = 7$ tens
$14 - 8 = 6$ ones

$$\begin{array}{r} {\scriptstyle 12} \\ {\scriptstyle 5\ \cancel{2}\ 14} \\ \cancel{6}\,\cancel{3}\,\cancel{4} \\ -\ 1\,5\,8 \\ \hline 4\,7\,6 \end{array}$$

In the method above, the numbers are ungrouped from right to left, but students can also ungroup from left to right. Children can choose whichever way works best for them. Once the ungrouping is completed, subtraction can also be performed either from right to left or from left to right.

Your child should also continue to practice multiplication and division skills at home.

If you have any questions or comments, please call or write me.

Sincerely,
Your child's teacher

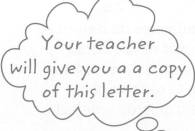

Your teacher will give you a a copy of this letter.

Carta a la familia

Estimada familia:

Ahora su niño está aprendiendo a restar. Un error muy común al restar es hacerlo en la dirección equivocada. Los niños pueden pensar que siempre se le resta el dígito más pequeño del dígito más grande, pero no es verdad. Para ayudar a los niños a no cometer este error, el programa *Math Expressions* les propone "arreglar" los números primero y luego restar.

$$\begin{array}{r} 634 \\ -\,158 \\ \hline 524 \end{array}$$

Cuando uno o más de los dígitos del número de arriba es más pequeño que el dígito correspondiente del número de abajo, se arreglan los números "desagrupándolos". Por ejemplo, 634 −158 se muestra abajo:

1. No podemos restar 8 unidades de 4 unidades. Obtenemos más unidades al desagrupar 1 decena para formar 10 unidades.

   Ahora tenemos 14 unidades y solamente 2 decenas.

$$\begin{array}{r} {}^{2\ 14} \\ 6\,3\,4 \\ -\,1\,5\,8 \end{array}$$

2. No podemos restar 5 decenas de 2 decenas. Obtenemos más decenas al desagrupar 1 centena para formar 10 decenas.

   Ahora tenemos 12 decenas y solamente 5 centenas.

$$\begin{array}{r} {}^{12} \\ {}^{5\ \,2\ 14} \\ 6\,3\,4 \\ -\,1\,5\,8 \end{array}$$

3. Ahora podemos restar:

   5 − 1 =
   4 centenas
   12 − 5 =
   7 decenas
   14 − 8 =
   6 unidades

$$\begin{array}{r} {}^{12} \\ {}^{5\ \,2\ 14} \\ 6\,3\,4 \\ -\,1\,5\,8 \\ \hline 4\,7\,6 \end{array}$$

En el método de arriba se desagrupan los números de derecha a izquierda, pero también se pueden desagrupar de izquierda a derecha. Los niños pueden escoger la manera que les resulte más fácil. Una vez que hayan desagrupado, la resta también puede hacerse de derecha a izquierda o de izquierda a derecha.

Su niño también debe seguir practicando las destrezas de multiplicación y de división en casa.

Si tiene alguna pregunta o comentario, por favor comuníquese conmigo.

Tu maestro te dará una copia de esta carta.

Atentamente,
El maestro de su niño

Subtract From Hundreds

Class Activity

▶ Draw and Solve Multi-Digit Addition

Addition and subtraction are **inverse operations**.
Break-apart drawings help to show inverse relationships.

1. Write a word problem that requires adding 257 and 143.

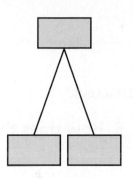

2. Write the **addends** in the break-apart drawing.

3. Discuss how this place-value drawing matches each
   addition method.

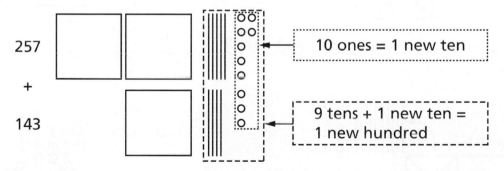

257

\+

143

10 ones = 1 new ten

9 tens + 1 new ten =
1 new hundred

New Groups Above	New Groups Below	Show Subtotals
$\begin{array}{r} 1\,1 \\ 257 \\ +\,143 \\ \hline 400 \end{array}$	$\begin{array}{r} 257 \\ +\,143 \\ \hline {\scriptstyle 1\,1} \\ 400 \end{array}$	$\begin{array}{r} 257 \\ +\,143 \\ \hline 300 \\ 90 \\ +\ \ 10 \\ \hline 400 \end{array}$

4. Copy and complete the break-apart drawing next to problem 1.

▶ Draw and Solve Multi-Digit Subtraction

5. Write a word problem that requires subtracting 257 from 400.

Discuss.

6. How does this drawing show ungrouping 1 hundred?

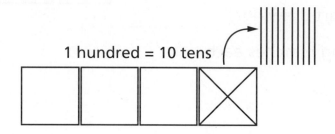

1 hundred = 10 tens

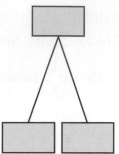

3 10
4̶ 0̶ 0
− 2 5 7

7. How does this drawing show ungrouping 1 ten?

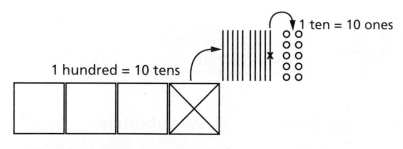

1 ten = 10 ones

1 hundred = 10 tens

9
3 1̶0 10
4̶ 0̶ 0̶
− 2 5 7

8. How does this drawing show the solution?

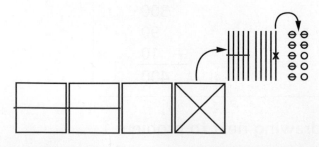

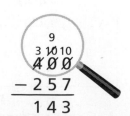

9
3 1̶0 10
4̶ 0̶ 0̶
− 2 5 7
1 4 3

9. Explain how you ungroup 200 to subtract 25.

10. How can you use subtraction to check addition?

▶ Describe Ungrouping

Look at 864 − 586.

1. Which number does the drawing represent?

$$\begin{array}{r} 864 \\ -\ 586 \end{array}$$

You can ungroup left-to-right as shown in problems 2 and 3
before you subtract.

2. Ungroup 1 hundred to see ⬛ more tens.

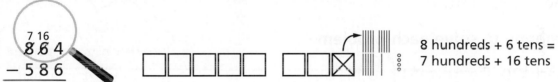

8 hundreds + 6 tens =
7 hundreds + 16 tens

3. Ungroup 1 ten to see ⬛ more ones.

16 tens + 4 ones =
15 tens + 14 ones

You can ungroup right-to-left as shown in problems 4 and 5
before you subtract.

4. Ungroup 1 ten to see ⬛ more ones.

6 tens + 4 ones =
5 tens + 14 ones

5. Ungroup 1 hundred to see ⬛ more tens.

8 hundreds + 5 tens =
7 hundreds + 15 tens

▶ Subtraction and Money

You can use models to help you subtract money amounts.

Sondra had $140 to spend on new clothes for school. She bought a shirt for $21. To find out how much money she had left, use play money to act out the problem.

Sondra had _____ left.

Use play money to solve each problem.

1. Jason had $30. He gave $18 to his brother. How much money does Jason have left?

2. Elana's coach had $250 to spend on softball equipment. She spent $76 on bases. How much does the coach have left?

3. The school science club raised $325. After buying equipment for an experiment they had $168 left. How much did they spend?

4. Amy paid $575 for new furniture. Before buying it she had $813. How much did she have afterward?

5. Mrs. Washington has $265. She wants to buy shoes for $67 and dresses for $184. Does she have enough money? Explain your answer.

Show your work on your paper or in your journal.

▶ Discuss Ungrouping With Zeros

Look inside the magnifying glass and discuss each ungrouping step.

1. Ungroup step-by-step: *or*

```
    9  9
  7 10 10 10
  8̸ 0̸ 0̸ 0̸
 − 3,4 9 2
```

2. Ungroup all at once:

```
  7  9  9 10
  8̸ 0̸ 0̸ 0̸
 − 3,4 9 2
```

▶ Decide When to Ungroup

3. Ungroup left-to-right: *or*

```
      15 11
  3 16 12 15
  4̸ 6̸ 2̸ 5̸
 − 2,9 8 7
```

4. Ungroup right-to-left:

```
      15 11
  3  8̸  1̸ 15
  4̸ 6̸ 2̸ 5̸
 − 2,9 8 7
```

▶ Other Ungrouping Situations

5. When we have zeros and other digits on the top:

```
  1 16  9 13
    8̸ 10
  2 7̸ 0̸ 3̸
 − 1,9 6 6
```

6. When we have the same digit on the top and bottom:

```
      13 17
  4 14  7 13
  5̸ 4̸ 8̸ 3̸
 − 1,6 8 7
```

7. On the Back Show how to subtract 4,238 from 5,003.

► Find and Correct Mistakes

Always check your work. Many mistakes can be easily fixed.

What is the mistake in each problem? How can you fix the mistake and find the correct answer?

1. 67,308 − 5,497

$$
\begin{array}{r}
{}^{12} \\
^{6}\,{}^{1\!3}\!\!{}^{10} \\
6\,7{,}\cancel{3}\,\cancel{0}\,8 \\
-\ \ 5{,}4\,9\,7 \\
\hline
1\,2{,}3\,3\,8
\end{array}
$$

2. 134,865 − 5,294

$$
\begin{array}{r}
134{,}865 \\
-\ \ \ 5{,}294 \\
\hline
131{,}631
\end{array}
$$

► Check Subtraction by "Adding Up"

"Add up" to find any places where there is a subtraction mistake. Discuss how each mistake might have been made and correct the subtraction if necessary.

3.
$$
\begin{array}{r}
163{,}406 \\
-\ 84{,}357 \\
\hline
79{,}159
\end{array}
$$

4.
$$
\begin{array}{r}
526{,}741 \\
-\ 139{,}268 \\
\hline
413{,}473
\end{array}
$$

5.
$$
\begin{array}{r}
2{,}380{,}043 \\
-\ \ 678{,}145 \\
\hline
1{,}701{,}908
\end{array}
$$

6.
$$
\begin{array}{r}
5{,}472{,}639 \\
-\ 2{,}375{,}841 \\
\hline
3{,}096{,}798
\end{array}
$$

7. Write and solve a subtraction problem with numbers in the millions.

▶ Estimate Differences

You can use estimation to decide if an answer is reasonable.

Dan did this subtraction: 8,196 − 5,980. His answer was 3,816. Discuss how using estimation can help you decide if his answer is correct.

Decide whether each answer is reasonable. Show your estimate.

1. 4,914 − 949 = 3,065

2. 52,022 − 29,571 = 22,451

Solve.

3. Bob has 3,226 marbles in his collection. Mia has 1,867 marbles. Bob says he has 2,359 more than Mia. Is Bob's answer reasonable? Show your estimate.

Show your work on your paper or in your journal.

4. Two towns have populations of 24,990 and 12,205. Gretchen says the difference is 12,785. Is Gretchen's answer reasonable? Show your estimate.

5. Estimate to decide if the answer is reasonable. If it is not reasonable, describe the mistake and find the correct answer.

$$\begin{array}{r} 8,005,716 \\ -\ 2,900,905 \\ \hline 6,104,811 \end{array}$$

▶ Use a Price List

School Supplies			
Pen	$0.19	Spiral notebook	$0.89
Pencil	$0.15	Loose-leaf paper (50 sheets)	$0.69
Colored markers (box of 8)	$1.49	Computer disk	$0.75
Pencil box	$0.70	Gym T-shirt	$3.50
Eraser	$0.15	Combination lock	$2.89

Answer each question. Explain your thinking.

Show your work on your paper or in your journal.

1. Sylvia has $5.00 to buy a T-shirt. Will she have enough left to buy a box of markers?

2. Bo has $4.00. How many computer disks can he buy?

3. Bilana has $4.00. She wants to buy a combination lock, pencil box, and a notebook. Does she have enough?

4. Joseph has $2.00. He wants to buy a pack of paper and 2 erasers. Can he also buy 5 ball-point pens?

5. **Math Journal** Use the price list to write two word problems.

▶ Use a Table With Larger Numbers

This table shows the total area of some U.S. National Parks in **acres** . (1 acre = 4,840 square yards)

Park Name	State	Total Acres
Big Bend	Texas	801,163
Canyonlands	Utah	337,598
Carlsbad Caverns	New Mexico	46,766
Channel Islands	California	249,561
Everglades	Florida	1,508,538
Gates of the Arctic	Alaska	8,472,506
Glacier	Montana	1,013,572
Grand Canyon	Arizona	1,217,403
Great Smoky Mountains	North Carolina/Tennessee	521,752
Isle Royale	Michigan	571,790
Mammoth Cave	Kentucky	52,830
Olympic	Washington	922,651
Shenandoah	Virginia	199,045

Use the table to solve each problem.

6. Which is greater, the area of Big Bend National Park or the combined area of Channel Islands and Isle Royale parks? Estimate the difference and explain your thinking.

Show your work on your paper or in your journal.

7. Which park is closest in area to the area of Canyonlands and Olympic parks combined?

Estimate With Real-World Situations

▶ Use a Table With Larger Numbers (continued)

Show your work on your paper or in your journal.

Use the table to solve each problem.

8. Estimate the total area of the three largest parks listed in the table. Show how you estimated.

9. What is the difference between the area of Great Smoky Mountains park and the area of Shenandoah park? Check your answer by rounding and estimating.

10. Which park is about 4 times the area of Carlsbad Caverns park? Use estimation and explain your thinking.

▶ Write Your Own Word Problems

11. **Math Journal** Research some real-world data with large numbers. Make a table of the data. Then write two or three word problems using your data.

Vocabulary

estimate

▶ Estimate or Exact Answer?

Decide whether you need an **estimate** or exact answer to solve each problem. Then solve the problem.

1. Miguel gave the clerk two $20 bills for a hat that cost $16.50 and a shirt that cost $12.00. How much change should Miguel receive?

2. Fairview Elementary has 564 students. Lincoln Elementary has 728 students. About how many students attend the two schools?

3. A school has a fundraising goal of selling 1,000 candles. They sell between 100 and 300 candles every day. How long will it take to meet their goal?

4. The Sanders family drove 421 miles to the beach. Coming home, they drove 366 miles to visit friends and then 207 miles home. About how many miles did they drive in all?

5. Sara wants a backpack that costs $38.95. She sees it on sale for $31.95 at a different store. How much cheaper is the backpack that is on sale?

Estimate With Real-World Situations

▶ Discuss Problem Types

Think of a change, collection, or comparison problem for each exercise. Write an equation for the problem then solve it.

1. $a + 278 = 747$

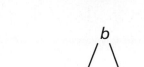

747
/\
a   278

2. $b - 346 = 587$

b
/\
346   587

3.

933
/\
c   346

4.

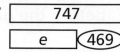

| 747 |
| e | 469 |

▶ Share Solutions

Write an equation for the problem then solve it.
Make a math drawing if you need to.

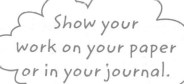

Show your work on your paper or in your journal.

5. Of 800,000 species of insects, about 560,000 undergo complete metamorphosis. How many species do not undergo complete metamorphosis?

6. The Great Pyramid of Giza has about 2,000,000 stone blocks. A replica has 1,900,000 fewer blocks. How many blocks are in the replica?

7. Last year 439,508 people visited Fun World. This is 46,739 fewer visitors than this year. How many people visited Fun World this year?

▶ **Share Solutions (continued)**

8. At the end of a baseball game, there were 35,602 people in the stadium. There were 37,614 people there at the beginning of the game. How many people left before the game ended?

9. This year Pinnacle Publishing printed 64,924 more books than Premier Publishing. If Pinnacle printed 231,069 books, how many did Premier print?

10. Mary drove her car 2,483 miles during a road trip. Now she has 86,445 miles on her car. How many miles did her car have before her trip?

11. The Elbe River in Europe is 1,170 km long. The Yellow River in China is 5,465 km long. How long are the two rivers altogether?

12. A bridge is 1,595 feet long. Each cable holding up the bridge is 1,983 feet longer than the bridge itself. How long is each cable?

▶ Math and Science

T. rex "Sue" is the largest *T. rex* dinosaur skeleton ever found. You can see Sue at The Field Museum in Chicago. The table below shows data about Sue and some animals that live on Earth today.

Name	Approximate Weight	Number of Teeth
T. Rex Sue	7 tons	58
Humpback whale	35–50 tons	0
African elephant	3–6 tons	24
Giant anteater	50–100 lb	0
Opossum	8–13 lb	50

1. Look at the data in the table. Is there is a relationship between the weight of the animals and the number of teeth they have? Use the data to support your answer.

2. Suppose you had a giant balance scale with a 35-ton humpback whale on one side. About how many dinosaurs the size of Sue would you have to put on the other side to balance the scale? Explain how you got your answer.

3. Write a question that can be answered by using the data in the table. Provide the answer to the question.

▶ Compare Sets of Data From a Survey

The graphs show the results of a survey. Everyone surveyed has either 1 dog or 1 cat. People in Group 1 live in an apartment, and people in Group 2 live in a house.

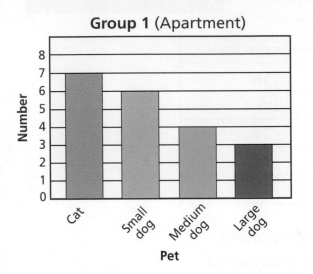

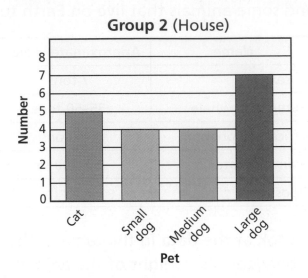

1. Make two statements that compare the data in the two groups.

2. Answer these questions to develop your own survey.

   • What question would you like to ask two groups of people?

   • What two groups of people will you survey?

   • What four answer choices will you have for your question?

3. Survey the two groups.

   • Record the responses in a tally chart.

   • Display the results for each group in its own bar graph.

   • Make two statements that compare data in the two groups.

Write an equation, using a letter to represent the unknown. Then solve.

> *Show your work on your paper or in your journal.*

1. Gaddi exercised 30 minutes on the weekend. She exercised a total of 95 minutes for the week. How many minutes did she exercise on the weekdays?

2. A trainer has 72 bottles of water to give away. By noon, he has 37 bottles of water. How many bottles of water did he give away before noon?

Make a break-apart drawing. Then write and solve an equation, using a letter to represent the unknown.

3. In a collection of 128 marbles, 19 marbles are red. How many marbles in the collection are not red?

Draw comparison bars. Write and solve an equation.

4. At the playground there are 5 slides. There are 7 more swings than slides. How many swings are there?

Solve each problem mentally or use equations, comparison bars, or break-apart drawings.

5. Thomas is thinking of a number. If 8 is added to his number and 6 is subtracted from that sum, the result is 12. What is the number?

6. Shana has a vase with 5 roses, 3 tulips, 14 carnations, and 23 daisies. How many more carnations than roses and tulips are in the vase?

Write the value of the underlined digit.

7. 59,<u>8</u>03

8. 8,7<u>7</u>4,002

Write each number in standard form.

9. seventy-five thousand, four hundred eight

10. five million, sixty-nine thousand, seven hundred thirty-six

Write >, <, or = to make each statement true.

11. 45,907 _____ 45,799

12. 728,925 _____ 729,825

Round to the nearest hundred.

13. 8,659

Round to the nearest thousand.

14. 37,808

Copy each exercise, lining up the places correctly. Then add or subtract.

15. 1,472 + 5,178 =

16. 25,097 + 57,336 =

17. 6,824 − 3,731 =

18. 57,875 − 43,088 =

19. 50,000 − 31,602 =

20. **Extended Response** Determine whether the following statement is true or false. Explain your thinking.

    6,421 − (284 + 653) = (6,421 − 284) + 653

► Discuss Angles

Angles can be many different sizes.

Discuss the groups of angles.

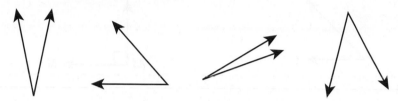

1. How are all these **acute angles** alike?

2. How is an acute angle different from a **right angle**?

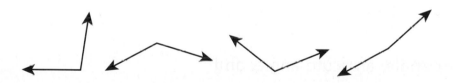

3. How are all of these **obtuse angles** alike?

4. How are they different from a right angle?

5. How are they different from an acute angle?

▶ Classify Angles

**Name each angle, using the letters. Label each angle as
right, acute, or obtuse.**

6. *F*

G → *H*

7. *X*

Y → *Z*

8. *L*

M → *N*

9. Use letters to name two acute and two obtuse angles in
   this figure. Label each as obtuse or acute.

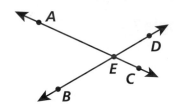

10. Draw and label a right angle, an acute angle, and
    an obtuse angle.

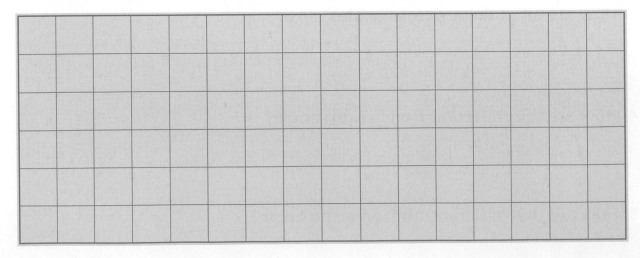

Vocabulary

protractor

▶ Use a Protractor

A **protractor** is a tool that is used to measure angles in degrees. This protractor shows that ∠ABC measures 90°.

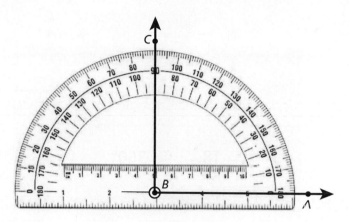

Measure each angle with your protractor. Write the measure.

11.

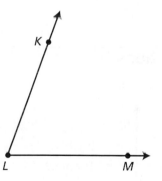

∠KLM = ▨

12.

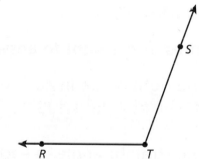

∠STR = ▨

13.

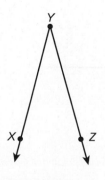

∠XYZ = ▨

14.

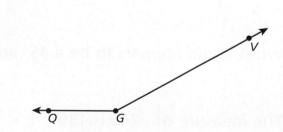

∠QGV = ▨

Show your work on your paper or in your Activity Workbook.

▶ Sketch Angles

Sketch each angle, or draw it using a protractor.

15. 90°

16. 45°

17. 180°

18. 360°

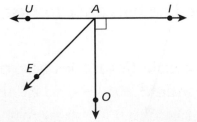

▶ Use Reasoning

Use the figures at the right to answer the following questions.

19. Name one right angle in each figure.

20. Name one straight angle in each figure.

21. How much greater is the measure of ∠KRB than the measure of ∠IAO?

22. What angle appears to be a 45° angle?

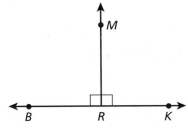

23. The measure of ∠IAE is 135°.

What is the measure of ∠OAE?

What is the measure of ∠UAE?

Naming and Measuring Angles

► Angles in the Real World

Here is a map of Jon's neighborhood. The east and west streets are named for presidents of the United States. The north and south streets are numbered. The avenues have letters. Jon's house is on the corner of Lincoln and First.

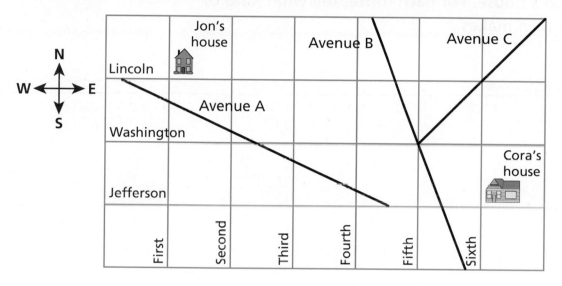

24. What do the arrows to the left of the map tell you?

25. Jon leaves his house and rides his bike south on First. What kind of angle does he make for each turn in this route?

   • He turns southeast onto avenue A.

   • When he reaches Washington, he turns west.

   • When he gets back to First, he turns south.

26. Jon's cousin Cora rides east on Lincoln from Jon's house to avenue C. What kind of angle will she make if she turns northeast? if she turns southwest?

► More Angles in the Real World

Look at the map of Jon's neighborhood on page 185.

27. Cora lives at the corner of Jefferson and Sixth. Record three different routes she can use to get from her house to Jon's house. For each route, tell what kind of angle each turn makes.

28. Write what you know about right, acute, and obtuse angles.

Dear Family,

This unit is your child's second short geometry unit. It is about the different kinds of triangles.

Right triangle

One right angle (90°)

Acute triangle

All angles less than 90°

Obtuse triangle

One angle greater than 90°

Equilateral triangle

All three sides congruent (equal size)

Isosceles triangle

Two sides congruent

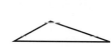

Scalene triangle

Three different sides

Your child will also discover the standard method for finding the perimeter of a triangle (side + side + side) and the area of a triangle ($\frac{1}{2}$ × base × height).

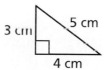

3 cm   5 cm

4 cm

Perimeter (P) = 3 cm + 4 cm + 5 cm = 12 cm

Area (A) = $\frac{1}{2}$ × 4 cm × 3 cm = 6 square cm

Be sure that your child continues to review and practice the basics of multiplication and division. A good understanding of the basics will be very important later in the year when students learn more difficult concepts in multiplication and division.

If you have any questions or comments, please call or write to me.

Thank you.

Sincerely,
Your child's teacher

Your teacher will give you a copy of this letter.

Estimada familia:

Ésta es la segunda unidad corta de geometría que ve su niño. Presenta diferentes tipos de triángulos.

Triángulo rectángulo

Tiene un ángulo recto (90°)

Triángulo acutángulo

Todos los ángulos son menores de 90°

Triángulo obtusángulo

Tiene un ángulo mayor de 90°

Triángulo equilátero

Los tres lados son congruentes (mismo tamaño)

Triángulo isósceles

Dos lados son congruentes

Triángulo escaleno

Los tres lados son diferentes

Su niño también aprenderá el método normal para hallar el perímetro de un triángulo (lado + lado + lado) y el área de un triángulo ($\frac{1}{2} \times$ base $\times$ altura).

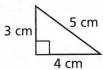

Perímetro (P) = 3 cm + 4 cm + 5 cm = 12 cm

Área (A) = $\frac{1}{2} \times$ 4 cm $\times$ 3 cm = 6 cm cuadrados

Asegúrese de que su niño siga repasando y practicando las multiplicaciones y divisiones básicas. Es importante que comprenda las operaciones básicas para que pueda aprender conceptos de multiplicación y división más difíciles.

Si tiene alguna pregunta o comentario, por favor comuníquese conmigo.

Gracias.

Atentamente,
El maestro de su niño

Tu maestro te dará una copia de esta carta.

Name Angles

▶ Identify Rotations

A **rotation** is a turn. A number of degrees (°) and a direction (clockwise or counter-clockwise) describe a turn.

1. Which answer choice shows the pencil after a 90° counter-clockwise turn?

a. b. c.

2. Which answer choice shows the figure after a 270° clockwise turn?

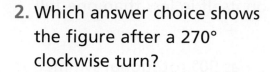

a. b. c.

3. Which answer choice shows the figure after a 90° clockwise turn?

a. b. c.

4. Which answer choice shows the figure after a 360° turn?

a. b. c.

5. One full turn is the same as how many half turns?

6. One full turn is the same as how many quarter turns?

7. How many degrees are in a circle?

Vocabulary

rotational symmetry

► Rotational Symmetry

A figure has **rotational symmetry** if you can turn it about its center and it fits exactly on itself in less than one full turn.

A square has 90° rotational symmetry because the first time it fits exactly on itself is after a quarter turn.

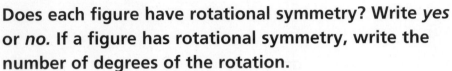

Does each figure have rotational symmetry? Write *yes* or *no*. If a figure has rotational symmetry, write the number of degrees of the rotation.

8.

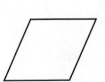

9.

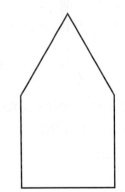

10.

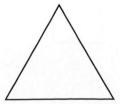

11.

4–3

Class Activity

Show your work on your paper or in your Activity Workbook.

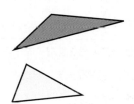

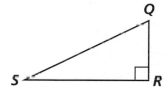

Vocabulary

right triangle
obtuse triangle
acute triangle

▶ **Discuss Angles of a Triangle**

The prefix *tri-* means "three," so it is easy to remember that a triangle has 3 angles. Triangles can take their names from the kind of angles they have.

• A **right triangle** has one right angle, which we show by drawing a small square at the right angle.

• An **obtuse triangle** has one obtuse angle.

• An **acute triangle** has three acute angles.

1. You can also use letters to write and talk about triangles. This triangle is △ *QRS*. Name its three angles and their type.

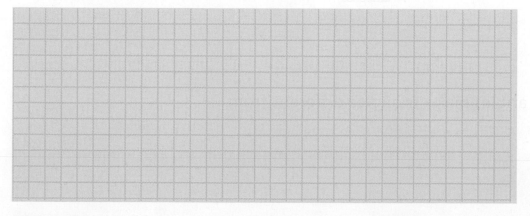

2. What kind of triangle is △ *QRS*? How do you know?

3. Draw and label a right triangle, an acute triangle, and an obtuse triangle.

► Identify Angles of a Triangle

Name each triangle by its angles. Explain your thinking.

4.

5.

6.

7.

8.

9.

10.

11.

12.

13.

14.

15.

16. Describe how angles make triangles different from
    one another.

Vocabulary

congruent
equilateral
isosceles
scalene

▶ Discuss Sides of a Triangle

Triangles can be named for their sides. Small perpendicular marks on the sides of triangles tell us when sides are **congruent**.

- The prefix *equi-* means "equal." Triangles that have three congruent sides are called **equilateral**.

- Triangles that have two congruent sides are called **isosceles**. The word *isosceles* comes from very old words that mean "equal legs."

- Triangles with no congruent sides are called **scalene**. All triangles that are not equilateral or isosceles are scalene.

Use these triangles to answer the questions.

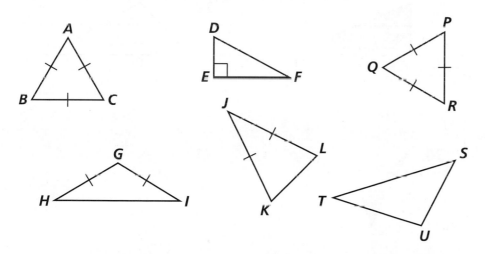

17. Write the letter names of the scalene triangles.

18. Write the letter names of the equilateral triangles.

19. Write the letter names of the isosceles triangles.

Class Activity

► Identify Sides of a Triangle

Name each triangle by its sides. Explain your thinking.

20.

21.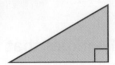

22.

23.

24.

25.

26.

27.

28.

29.

30.

31.

32. Explain how sides make triangles different from each other.

Name Triangles

Show your work on your paper or in your Activity Workbook.

▶ Possible Ways to Name Triangles

33. Can triangles be named for both their sides and their angles? Explain your thinking.

Draw each triangle. If you can't, explain why.

34. Draw a right scalene triangle.	35. Draw an obtuse scalene triangle.
36. Draw a right equilateral triangle.	37. Draw an acute isosceles triangle.
38. Draw an obtuse equilateral triangle.	39. Draw a right isosceles triangle.

Going Further

Cut out shapes from your Activity Workbook.

▶ **Sort Triangles in Different Ways**

Write a capital letter and a lowercase letter inside each triangle, using the keys to the right.

Cut out the triangles and use the Venn diagram to sort them in different ways.

| acute = a |
| obtuse = o |
| right = r |

| Isosceles = I |
| Scalene = S |
| Equilateral = E |

Triangles

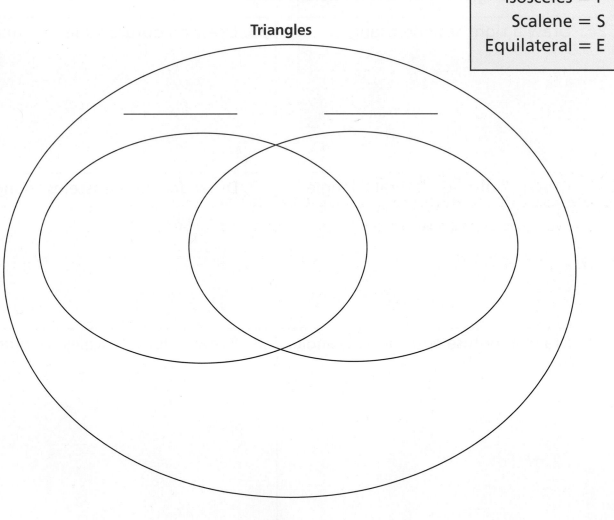

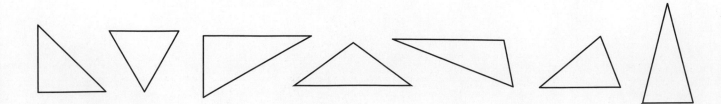

Name Triangles

Cut out shapes from your Activity Workbook.

Vocabulary

quadrilateral
congruent

▶ Build Quadrilaterals With Triangles

You can make a **quadrilateral** by joining two **congruent** triangles together along corresponding sides.

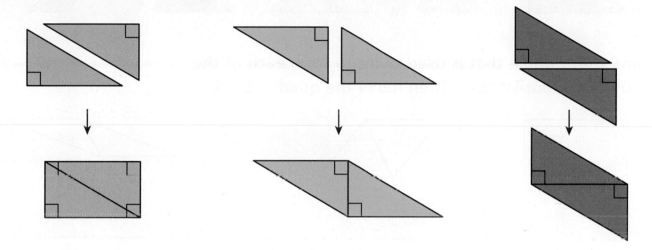

Cut out the congruent triangles. For each exercise, glue two of the triangles on paper so that the stated sides are joined. Then write the name of the quadrilateral.

1. *AB* is joined to *AB*   **2.** *AC* is joined to *AC*   **3.** *BC* is joined to *BC*

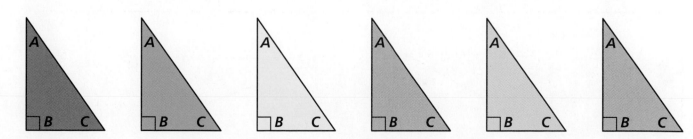

Triangles and Diagonals **197**

► Match Quadrilaterals With Triangles

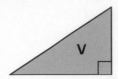 V   W   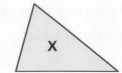 X   Y   Z

Name the triangle that is used twice to form each of the following quadrilaterals. Then name the quadrilateral.

4.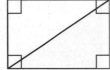

5.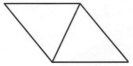

6.

7.

8.

9.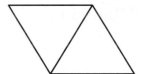

► Make Triangles With Diagonals

A **diagonal** connects opposite angles of a quadrilateral. You can make triangles by drawing a diagonal on a quadrilateral.

Name each quadrilateral. Then use letters to name the triangles you can make with the diagonals.

10.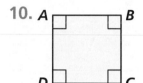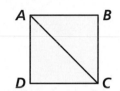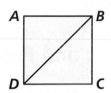

11.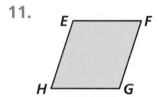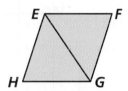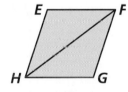

12.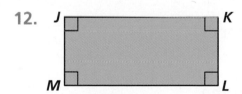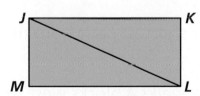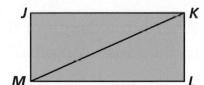

13.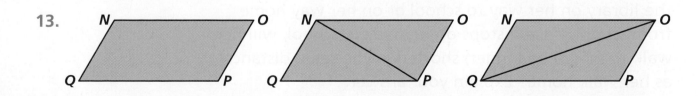

Show your work on your paper or in your Activity Workbook.

▶ **Arrays and Paths**

1. Connect the dots in each figure without lifting your
   pencil or crossing over a line.

▶ **Maps and Paths**

Each square on the grid below represents 1 block.
Use the grid to answer the questions that follow.

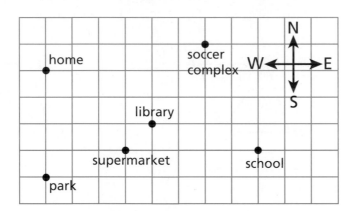

2. What is the length of the shortest path from the park
   to the soccer complex?

3. Where will Leah be if she walks 4 blocks west from the
   library, and then walks 2 blocks north?

4. Leah is leaving home to walk to school. She must stop at
   the library on her way to school or on her way home
   from school. If Leah stops on her way to school, will her
   walk to school be longer, shorter, or the same distance
   as her walk home? Explain your answer.

Class Activity

▶ Find the Perimeter of Triangles

Think about what you already know about finding perimeter. Discuss a method that will work to find the perimeter of each quadrilateral.

1.

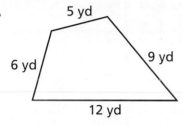

5 yd
6 yd
9 yd
12 yd

2.

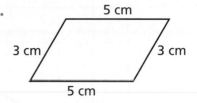

5 cm
3 cm
3 cm
5 cm

3.

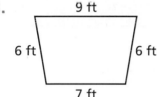

9 ft
6 ft
6 ft
7 ft

4.

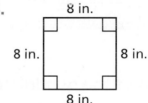

8 in.
8 in.
8 in.
8 in.

5. Which method will work for any quadrilateral?

6. Will a similar method work to find the perimeter of any triangle? Why?

Tell what other methods will work to find the perimeter of each of these triangles. Solve.

7.

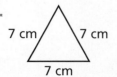

7 cm
7 cm
7 cm

8.

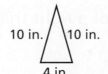

10 in.
10 in.
4 in.

9.

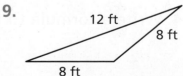

12 ft
8 ft
8 ft

Show your work on your paper or in your Activity Workbook.

Vocabulary

area

▶ Find the Area of Right Triangles

10. Draw a congruent triangle along the side marked *d* and write the name of the quadrilateral this makes.

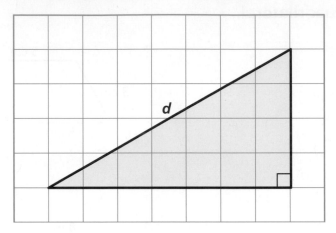

11. What is the **area** of the quadrilateral?
    What is half of that number?

12. What figure is half of the quadrilateral?
    What is the area of that figure?

13. Which triangle measurement did you not use? Why?

14. Write a formula to find the area of a right triangle.

Class Activity

Show your work on your paper or in your Activity Workbook.

▶ Find the Area of Other Triangles

15. Draw a congruent triangle along the side marked *d*. Write the name of the quadrilateral this makes.

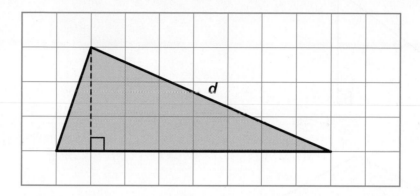

16. What measurement does the dotted line represent in the triangle above?

17. Why do you need the height to find the area of the quadrilateral?

18. Why do you also need the height to find the area of the triangle?

19. Write a formula to find the area of any triangle.

Class Activity

▶ Find Perimeter and Area of Triangles

Use your centimeter ruler to measure each triangle.
Then find its perimeter and area.

20.

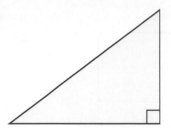

21.

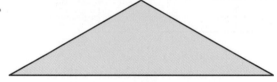

22.

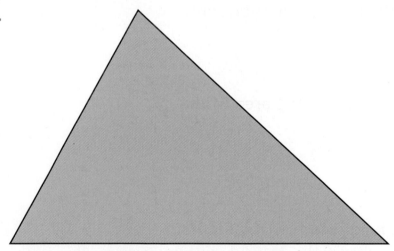

23.

Class Activity

Vocabulary

polygon
closed
regular
congruent

► What Are Polygons?

The prefix *poly-* means "many," and the suffix *-gon* refers to angles. A **polygon** has "many angles."

A polygon has only straight line segments that do not cross each other. A polygon is **closed**. That means it has no endpoints.

1. Circle the figures that are polygons.

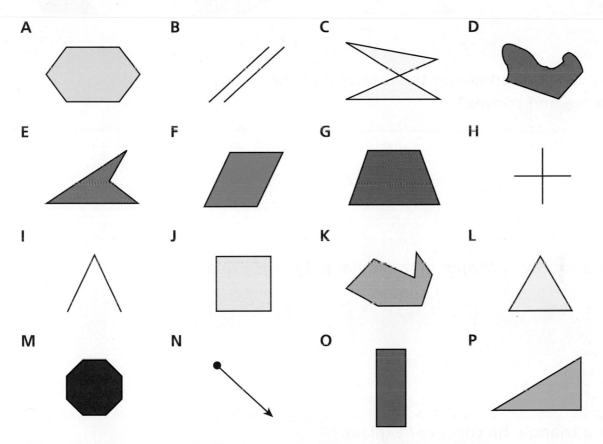

2. Why must a polygon have three or more sides and angles?

All sides and angles of a **regular** polygon are **congruent**.

3. Which of the polygons above look regular?

Vocabulary
convex
concave

▶ Convex and Concave Polygons

Polygons can be **convex** or **concave**. In a convex polygon, all of the diagonals are inside the polygon. In a concave polygon, at least one diagonal is outside the polygon.

Which polygons are convex and which are concave?

4. 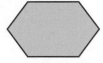   5.    6.   7.

8. How can you remember the meaning of the words concave and convex?

9. Can a concave polygon be a regular polygon? Explain.

10. Can a triangle be concave? Explain.

11. What is the common name for a regular 4-sided polygon?

12. What is the common name for a regular 3-sided polygon?

Polygons

► **Name Polygons**

Vocabulary

triangle
quadrilateral
pentagon

Polygons have special names that tell how many sides and angles they have. Some names of polygons are **triangle**, **quadrilateral**, and **pentagon**.

Write a prefix to match each number.

13. three   **14.** four   **15.** five

16. six   **17.** seven   **18.** eight

19. nine   **20.** ten   **21.** twelve

Name each polygon.

22.

23.

24.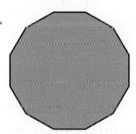

25.

26.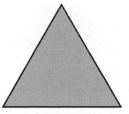

27.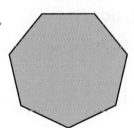

28.

29.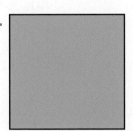

30.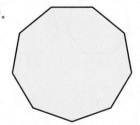

▶ Find Perimeter of Polygons

Use multiplication to write a general equation for the perimeter of each regular polygon. Use *P* to represent perimeter.

31. equilateral triangle

32. square

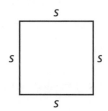

33. regular pentagon

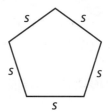

34. a regular hexagon with sides of length *s*

35. a regular dodecagon with sides of length *s*

36. Write a general equation for any regular polygon with *n* sides of length *s*.

What is the total perimeter of each group of regular polygons?

37.

6 cm   6 cm

38.

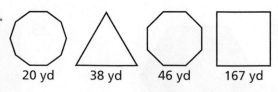

7 in.   7 in.   5 in.   5 in.

39.

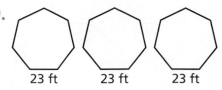

23 ft   23 ft   23 ft

40.

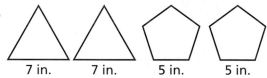

20 yd   38 yd   46 yd   167 yd

▶ Rotations About a Point

A **transformation** is a change in the position of a figure. An example of a transformation is a rotation. A **rotation** is a turn. Previously you learned that a figure can be rotated around a point that is in the center of the figure.

Show your work on your paper or in your Activity Workbook.

Vocabulary

transformation
rotation

Other ways to turn a figure include rotating it about a point that is on the figure, and rotating it about a point that is outside the figure.

inside the figure   on the figure   outside the figure

 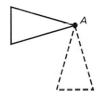

Each of the figures above shows a 90° clockwise rotation about Point *A*.

Complete these exercises.

1. Draw a 90° clockwise rotation about Point *A*.

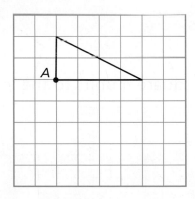

2. Draw a 180° clockwise rotation about Point *B*.

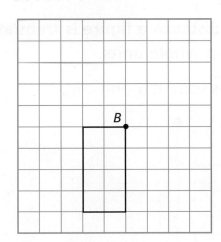

3. A three-quarter rotation is equal to how many degrees? Explain how you know.

Class Activity

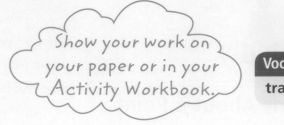
Show your work on your paper or in your Activity Workbook.

Vocabulary

translation

▶ Draw Translations

A **translation** is the movement of a figure along a straight line. Another name for a translation is a slide.

When a figure is translated, it moves along a line. The line may be horizontal or vertical. Figures may also be translated along lines that are not horizontal and not vertical.

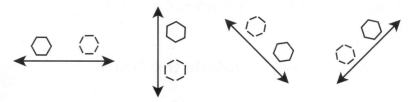

Draw the result of each translation.

4. Slide this square to the right.

5. Slide this square down.

The exact distance a figure is translated is sometimes described in whole units.

6. Slide this square 5 units up.

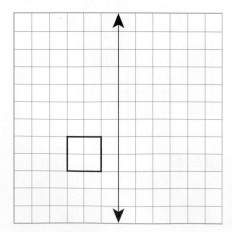

7. Slide this square 4 units to the left.

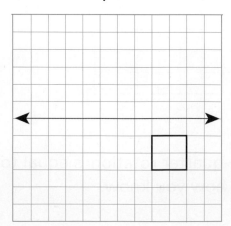

Class Activity

Show your work on your paper or in your Activity Workbook.

Vocabulary
reflection

► Draw Reflections

Previously you learned that rotations (or turns) and translations (or slides) were examples of transformations. Another kind of transformation is a reflection.

A **reflection** is the movement of a figure across a line, producing a mirror or congruent image of the figure.

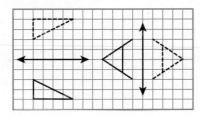

Reflect each figure across the given line.

8.

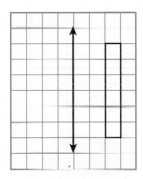

9.

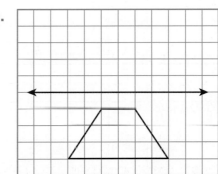

10.

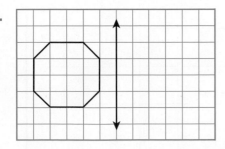

11.

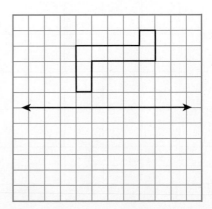

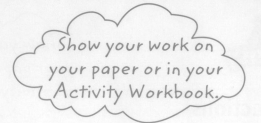

Show your work on your paper or in your Activity Workbook.

▶ **Grid Paper**

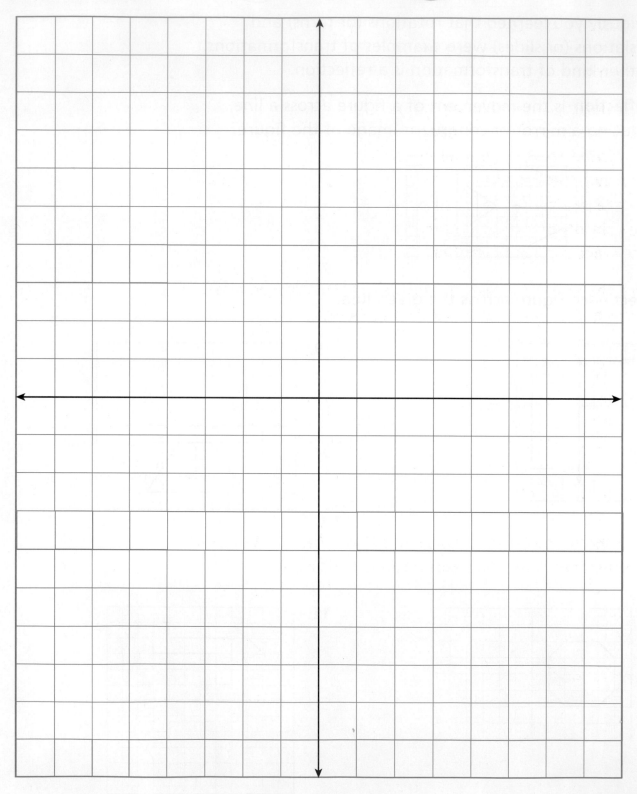

Transformations

▶ Transformations and Congruent Figures

Vocabulary

transformation
congruent

You have learned that a **transformation** is a change in the position of a figure.

A translation, reflection, or rotation of a figure produces an image that is congruent to the original figure. When two figures are **congruent**, they are exactly the same size and shape. In other words, one figure is an exact copy of the other.

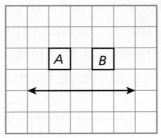

We can use a translation to show that these figures are congruent.

Write the name of *one* transformation that can be used to prove that Figure *B* is congruent to Figure *A*.

12.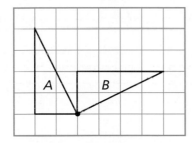

13.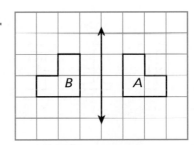

Write the name of *two* transformations that can be used to prove that Figure *B* is congruent to Figure *A*.

14.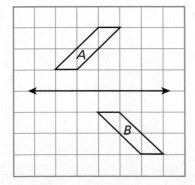

15.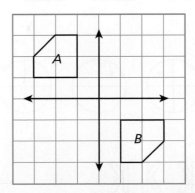

▶ Extend Patterns

The rules for some patterns can be described by
transformations. For example, when you view the pattern
below beginning at the left, the letter U rotates 90°
clockwise as you move from one letter to the next.

For each pattern of shapes below, use the word
translation, rotation, or *reflection* to describe the rule.
Then draw the figure that comes next.

1.

2.

3.

4.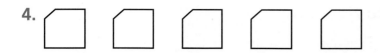

5.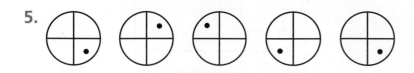

6. K K K K K

Transformations

Show your work on your paper or in your Activity Workbook.

Name each triangle by its angles. Explain your thinking.

1.

2.

3.

4. Use these triangles to answer the questions.

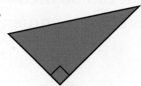 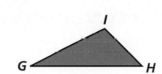 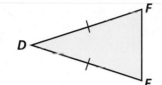

   A. Write the letter name of the scalene triangle.

   B. Write the letter name of the equilateral triangle.

5. Draw a diagonal. Describe the triangles formed.

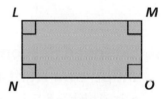

6. Which figure has 90° rotational symmetry. Explain.

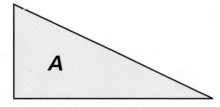

7. Find the perimeter and area.

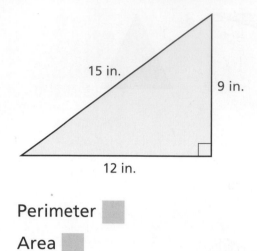

15 in.

9 in.

12 in.

Perimeter ▢

Area ▢

8. Write the name of one transformation that can be used to prove that Figure *B* is congruent to Figure *A*.

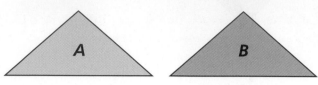

A   B

Show your work on your paper or in your journal.

9. James is making a patch for his jacket. The patch is a regular hexagon that measures 6 inches on each side. If he puts red cord around the perimeter of the patch, how much cord will he use?

10. **Extended Response** Farida is making a pennant in the shape of a right triangle. It has a base of 12 inches and a height of 5 inches. Its other side is 13 inches long. If Farida cuts the pennant out of a 15-inch square of felt, how many square inches of felt does she have left? Make a sketch and explain your thinking.

Class Activity

▶ Model a Product of Ones

Vocabulary

array
area

The number of unit squares in an **array**. of connected unit squares is the **area** of the rectangle formed by the squares. We sometimes just show the measurement of length and width.

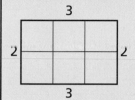 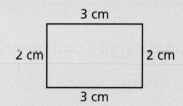

You can draw a rectangle for any multiplication. In the real world, we use multiplication for finding both sizes of arrays and areas of figures.

A 2 × 3 rectangle has 6 unit squares inside, so 2 × 3 = 6.

1. On your MathBoard, draw a 3 × 2 rectangle. How is the 3 × 2 rectangle similar to the 2 × 3 rectangle? How is it different?

2. How do the areas of the 2 × 3 and 3 × 2 rectangles compare?

▶ Factor the Tens to Multiply Ones and Tens

This 2 × 30 rectangle contains 6 groups of 10 square units, so its area is 60 square units.

```
30 =      10        +        10        +        10
1  | 1 × 10 = 10  |  1 × 10 = 10  |  1 × 10 = 10  | 1 . . .
1  | 1 × 10 = 10  |  1 × 10 = 10  |  1 × 10 = 10  | 1 . . .
. . . . 10 . . . + . . . 10 . . . + . . . 10 . . . . . .
```

3. How can we show this numerically? Complete the steps.

$2 \times 30 = (2 \times 1) \times (\underline{} \times 10)$

$= (\underline{} \times \underline{}) \times (1 \times 10)$

$= \underline{} \times 10 = 60$

4. On your MathBoard, draw a 30 × 2 rectangle and find its area.

5. How is the 30 × 2 rectangle similar to the 2 × 30 rectangle? How is it different?

6. Write out the steps for finding 4 × 20 by factoring the tens. Use your MathBoard if you need to.

Show your work on your paper or in your Activity Workbook.

▶ Model a Product of Tens

7. Find the area of this 20 × 30 rectangle by dividing it into 10-by-10 squares of 100.

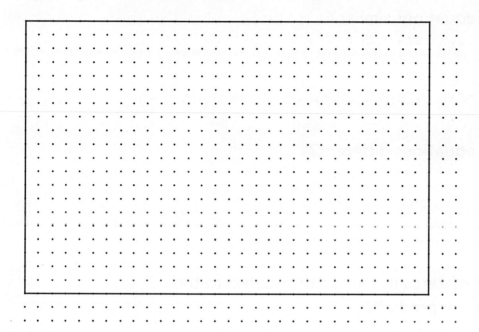

▶ Factor the Tens

8. Complete the steps to show your work in problem 7 numerically.

$$20 \times 30 = (\underline{} \times 10) \times (\underline{} \times 10)$$
$$= (\underline{} \times \underline{}) \times (10 \times 10)$$
$$= \underline{} \times 100$$
$$= 600$$

9. Is it true that 20 × 30 = 30 × 20? Explain how you know.

10. Write out the steps for finding 40 × 20 by factoring the tens. Use your MathBoard if you need to.

▶ **Compare Equations**

In this lesson, you looked at these three equations.

$$2 \times 3 = 6 \qquad 2 \times 30 = 60 \qquad 20 \times 30 = 600$$

11. How are the three equations similar?

12. How are the three equations different?

13. How is the number of zeros in the factors related to the number of zeros in the product?

Dear Family,

In this unit, your child will be learning about the common multiplication method that most adults know. However, they will also explore ways to draw multiplication. *Math Expressions* uses area of rectangles to show multiplication.

	30	+	7
20	20 × 30 = 600		20 × 7 = 140
+			
4	4 × 30 = 120		4 × 7 = 28

Area Method:

20 × 30 = 600
20 × 7 = 140
4 × 30 = 120
4 × 7 = 28
Total = 888

Shortcut Method:

$\overset{1}{\underset{2}{3}}7$
× 24
148
74
888

Area drawings help all students see multiplication. They also help students remember what numbers they need to multiply and what numbers make up the total.

Your child will also learn to find products involving single-digit numbers, tens, and hundreds by factoring the tens or hundreds. For example,

200 × 30 = 2 × 100 × 3 × 10
= 2 × 3 × 100 × 10
= 6 × 1,000 = 6,000

By observing the zeros patterns in products like these, your child will learn to do such multiplications mentally.

If your child is still not confident with single digit multiplication and division, we urge you to set aside a few minutes every night for multiplication and division practice. In a few more weeks, the class will be doing multi-digit division, so it is very important that your child be both fast and accurate with basic multiplication and division.

If you need practice materials, please contact your child's teacher.

Sincerely,
Your child's teacher

Your teacher will give you a a copy of this letter.

Carta a la familia

Estimada familia:

En esta unidad, su niño estará aprendiendo el método de multiplicación común que la mayoría de los adultos conoce. Sin embargo, también explorará maneras de dibujar la multiplicación. Para mostrar la multiplicación, *Math Expressions* usa el método del área del rectángulo.

	30	+	7
20	$20 \times 30 = 600$		$20 \times 7 = 140$
+			
4	$4 \times 30 = 120$		$4 \times 7 = 28$

Método del área

$20 \times 30 = 600$
$20 \times 7 = 140$
$4 \times 30 = 120$
$4 \times 7 = 28$
Total $= 888$

Método más corto

$$\overset{\overset{1}{2}}{37}$$
$$\underline{\times\ 24}$$
$$148$$
$$\underline{74}$$
$$888$$

Los dibujos de área ayudan a todos los estudiantes a visualizar la multiplicación. También ayudan a que los estudiantes recuerden qué números tienen que multiplicar y qué números forman el total.

Su niño también aprenderá a hallar productos a partir de números de un solo dígito, decenas y centenas factorizando las decenas o las centenas. Por ejemplo:

$$200 \times 30 = 2 \times 100 \times 3 \times 10$$
$$= 2 \times 3 \times 100 \times 10$$
$$= 6 \times 1,000 = 6,000$$

Al observar los patrones de ceros en productos como éstos, su niño aprenderá a hacer dichas multiplicaciones mentalmente.

Si su niño todavía no domina la multiplicación y la división con números de un solo dígito, le rogamos que le dedique algunos minutos todas las noches para practicar la multiplicación y la división. Dentro de pocas semanas, la clase hará divisiones con números de varios dígitos, por eso es muy importante que su niño haga las operaciones básicas de multiplicación y de división de manera rápida y exacta.

Si necesita materiales para practicar, comuníquese conmigo.

Atentamente,
El maestro de su niño

Tu maestro te dará una copia de esta carta.

Multiplication Arrays

Vocabulary

factor
product

▶ Look for Patterns

Multiplying large numbers in your head is easier when you learn patterns of multiplication with tens.

Start with column A and look for the patterns used to get the expressions in each column. Copy and complete the table.

Table 1

	A	B	C	D
	2 × 3	2 × 1 × 3 × 1	6 × 1	6
1.	2 × 30	2 × 1 × 3 × 10	6 × 10	▨
2.	20 × 30	2 × 10 × 3 × 10	▨	▨

3. How are the expressions in column B different from the expressions in column A?

4. In column C, we see that each expression can be written as a number times a place value. Which of these **factors** gives more information about the size of the **product**?

5. Why is 6 the first digit of the products in column D?

6. Why are there different numbers of zeros in the products in column D?

▶ **Compare Tables**

Copy and complete each table.

Table 2

	A	B	C	D
	6 × 3	6 × 1 × 3 × 1	18 × 1	18
7.	6 × 30	6 × 1 × 3 × 10	18 × 10	■
8.	60 × 30	6 × 10 × 3 × 10	■	■

Table 3

	A	B	C	D
	5 × 8	5 × 1 × 8 × 1	40 × 1	40
9.	5 × 80	5 × 1 × 8 × 10	40 × 10	■
10.	50 × 80	■	■	■

11. Why do the products in Table 2 have more digits than the products in Table 1?

12. Why are there more zeros in the products in Table 3 than those in Table 2?

► Explore the Area Model

Vocabulary
area
square units

20   +   6

4

1. How many **square units** of **area** are there in the tens part of the drawing?

2. What multiplication equation gives the area of the tens part of the drawing? Write this equation in its rectangle.

3. How many square units of area are there in the ones part?

4. What multiplication equation gives the area of the ones part? Write this equation in its rectangle.

5. What is the total of the two areas?

6. How do you know that 104 is the correct product of 4×26?

7. Read problems A and B.

   A. Al's photo album has 26 pages. Each page has 4 photos. How many photos are in Al's album?

   B. Nick took 4 photos. Henri took 26 photos. How many more photos did Henri take than Nick?

   Which problem could you solve using the multiplication you just did? Explain why.

Class Activity

▶ Use Rectangles to Multiply

Draw a rectangle for each problem on your MathBoard.
Find the tens product, the ones product, and the total.

8. 3 × 28

9. 3 × 29

10. 5 × 30

11. 5 × 36

12. 4 × 38

13. 8 × 38

14. 4 × 28

15. 5 × 28

Solve each problem.

16. Maria's father planted 12 rows of tomatoes in his garden. Each row had 6 plants. How many tomato plants were in Maria's father's garden?

17. The bakery can ice their cakes with chocolate, strawberry, or vanilla icing. The bakery has a total of 67 different ways to decorate iced cakes. How many different combinations of icing and decorations can the bakery make?

18. Complete this word problem. Then solve it.

_____ has _____ boxes of _____.

There are _____ _____ in each box.

How many _____ does _____

have altogether? _____

Show your work on your paper or in your journal.

Model One-Digit by Two-Digit Multiplication

Going Further

▶ Multiply One-Digit Dollar Amounts by Two-Digit Numbers

You can use your skills for multiplying a one-digit number by a two-digit number to multiply one-digit dollar amounts by two-digit numbers.

Find the exact cost. Give your answer in dollars.

Show your work on your paper or in your journal.

1. A package of paper costs $2. If someone is purchasing 24 packages, how much will it cost?

2. A box lunch can be purchased for $3. How much will 83 lunches cost?

3. A movie ticket costs $8 per person. If 61 people go to the five o'clock show, how much money does the theater make for that show?

4. A round-trip train ticket is $4 per person. If 58 fourth-graders take a field trip to the city on the train, how much will the train tickets cost?

5. The admission to the zoo is $5 per person. If a group of 72 students takes a field trip to the zoo, how much will their tickets cost altogether?

6. Sara earns $9 per hour as a cashier. How much does she earn in a 40-hour week?

Going Further

▶ Multiply Two-Digit Dollar Amounts by One-Digit Numbers

You can use your skills for multiplying a one-digit number by a two-digit number to multiply one-digit numbers by two-digit dollar amounts.

Find the exact cost. Give your answer in dollars.

Show your work on your paper or in your journal.

7. A bike costs $53. If 2 bikes are purchased, how much will be the total cost?

8. A store sells CDs for $14. If someone buys 7 of them, how much will they cost altogether?

9. An amusement park entrance fee is $23 per person. If 4 friends go to the amusement park, how much will their tickets cost altogether?

10. A hotel costs $72 per night. How much will it cost to stay 3 nights?

11. An airplane ticket costs $87. How much will 6 tickets cost?

12. Jorge earns $99 each week. He goes on vacation in 9 weeks. How much will he earn before his vacation?

Class Activity

▶ **Estimate Products**

Vocabulary

estimate
rounding

It is easier to **estimate** the product of a two-digit number and a one-digit number when you think about the two multiples of ten close to the two-digit number. This is shown in the drawings below.

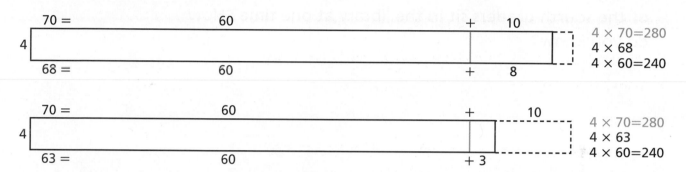

1. In each drawing, find the rectangles that represent 4×70 and 4×60. These rectangles "frame" the rectangles for 4×63 and 4×68. Find the values of 4×70 and 4×60.

   $4 \times 70 = $ ⬚ $4 \times 60 = $ ⬚

2. Look at the rectangle that represents 4×68. Is 4×68 closer to 4×60 or to 4×70? So is 4×68 closer to 240 or 280?

3. Look at the rectangle that represents 4×63. Is 4×63 closer to 4×60 or to 4×70? Is 4×63 closer to 240 or 280?

4. Explain how to use **rounding** to estimate the product of a one-digit number and a two-digit number.

► **Practice Estimation**

**Discuss how rounding and estimation could help solve
these problems.**

5. Keesha's school has 185 fourth-grade students. The
   library has 28 tables with 6 chairs at each table. Can all
   of the fourth-graders sit in the library at one time? How
   do you know?

6. Ameena is printing the class newsletter. There are
   8 pages in the newsletter, and she needs 74 copies. Each
   package of paper contains 90 sheets. How many
   packages of paper does she need to print the
   newsletter?

Estimate each product. Then solve to check your estimate.

7. 3×52

8. 7×48

9. 9×27

10. 8×34

11. 8×35

12. 5×22

▶ Numeric Multiplication Methods

You have used the area model to help you multiply.
In this lesson, you will learn some numeric multiplication
methods that are related to this area model.

Expanded Notation Method

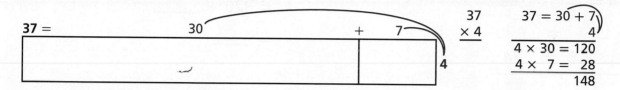

$$37 = 30 + 7$$

	37	$37 = 30 + 7$
	$\times\ 4$	$\underline{\qquad\qquad 4}$

$$4 \times 30 = 120$$
$$\underline{4 \times\ \ 7 =\ \ 28}$$
$$148$$

Algebraic Notation Method

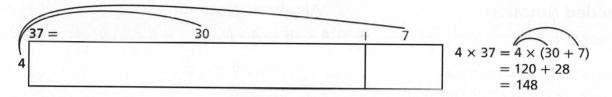

$$4 \times 37 = 4 \times (30 + 7)$$
$$= 120 + 28$$
$$= 148$$

▶ Connect the Multiplication Methods

Refer to the examples above.

1. What two values are added together to give the answer
   in the Expanded Notation Method?

2. What two values are added together to give the answer
   in the Algebraic Notation Method?

3. Choose one of the numeric methods and explain how it
   relates to the Rectangle Sections Method.

▶ Practice Different Methods

Fill in the blanks in the following solutions.

4. 4×86

Expanded Notation

$$86 = \underline{} + 6$$
$$\times\ 4 = \underline{}$$
$$4 \times \underline{} = \underline{}$$
$$\underline{} \times 6 = 24$$
$$\underline{}$$

Algebraic Notation

$$4 \cdot 86 = \underline{} \cdot (80 + 6)$$
$$= 320 + \underline{}$$
$$= \underline{}$$

5. 4×68

Expanded Notation

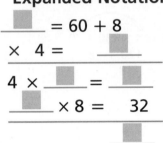

$$\underline{} = 60 + 8$$
$$\times\ 4 = \underline{}$$
$$4 \times \underline{} = \underline{}$$
$$\underline{} \times 8 = 32$$
$$\underline{}$$

Algebraic Notation

$$4 \cdot 68 = 4 \cdot (\underline{} + \underline{})$$
$$= 240 + \underline{}$$
$$= \underline{}$$

Solve using a numeric method. Sketch a rectangle if necessary.

6. $5 \times 64 = $

7. $6 \times 72 = $

8. $7 \times 92 = $

9. $8 \times 53 = $

10. $5 \times 46 = $

11. $6 \times 27 = $

Class Activity

► Compare Multiplication Methods

Compare these methods for solving 9 × 28.

Method A	Method B	Method C	Method D	Method E
$28 = 20 + 8$	$28 = 20 + 8$	28	28	$\overset{7}{28}$
$\underline{\times\ \ 9 =\qquad 9}$	$\underline{\times\ \ 9 =\qquad 9}$	$\underline{\times\ \ 9}$	$\underline{\times\ \ 9}$	$\underline{\times\ 9}$
$9 \times 20 = 180$	180	180	72	252
$\underline{9 \times 8 =\ \ 72}$	$\underline{\qquad\ \ 72}$	$\underline{\qquad 72}$	$\underline{\qquad 180}$	
252	252	252	252	

1. How are all the methods similar? List at least two similarities.

2. How are the methods different? List at least three differences.

► Analyze the Shortcut Method

Method E can be broken down into 2 steps.

Method E:	Step 1	Step 2
	$\overset{7}{28}$	$\overset{7}{28}$
	$\underline{\times\ 9}$	$\underline{\times\ 9}$
	2	252

3. Where are the products 180 and 72 from methods A–D?

5-6
Class Activity

▶ **Practice Multiplication**

Solve using any method. Sketch a rectangle if necessary.
Check your answer by rounding and estimating.

4. $5 \times 63 =$ ■

5. $39 \times 8 =$ ■

6. $98 \times 2 =$ ■

7. $4 \times 86 =$ ■

8. $7 \times 25 =$ ■

9. $47 \times 9 =$ ■

10. $3 \times 72 =$ ■

11. $6 \times 54 =$ ■

Discuss Different Methods

▶ Compare the Three Methods

You can use the **Rectangle Sections Method** to multiply a
one-digit number by a three-digit number.

237 =	200	+ 30	+ 7
4	4 × 200 = 800	4 × 30 = 120	4 × 7 = 28	4

$$\begin{array}{r} 800 \\ 120 \\ + \ 28 \\ \hline 948 \end{array}$$

1. What are the two steps used to find the product of
4 × 237 using the Rectangle Sections Method.

The **Expanded Notation Method** uses the same steps as the
Rectangle Sections Method.

237 =	200	+ 30	+ 7
4				4

$$237 = 200 + 30 + 7$$
$$\times \ 4 = \qquad\qquad 4$$
$$4 \times 200 = 800$$
$$4 \times 30 = 120$$
$$\underline{4 \times 7 = \ 28}$$
$$948$$

2. What is the last step in the Expanded Notation Method
and the Rectangle Sections Method?

The **Algebraic Notation Method** uses expanded notation
just like the other two methods. Even though the steps look
different, they are the same as in the other methods.

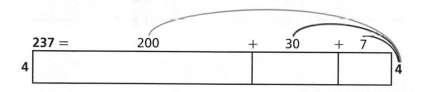

237 =	200	+ 30	+ 7
4				4

$$4 \cdot 237 = 4 \cdot (200 + 30 + 7)$$
$$= (4 \cdot 200) + (4 \cdot 30) + (4 \cdot 7)$$
$$= 800 + 120 + 28$$
$$= 948$$

3. What is the first step in all three methods?

Going Further

▶ Problem Solving With Money

You can use methods for multiplying a one-digit number by a three-digit number to multiply a money amount by a whole number.

Find the exact cost. Give your answer in cents and then give it in dollars.

Show your work on your paper or in your journal.

1. A one-hour paddleboat rental costs $9.95. How much would it cost to rent 6 paddleboats for an hour?

2. A salad bar costs $8.25. How much would it cost for a family of four to eat at the salad bar?

3. A can of cat food costs $0.79. How much do 9 cans cost?

4. A club is making tie-dyed T-shirts from white T-shirts. A package of 5 white T-shirts costs $5.29. How much would it cost to purchase 7 packages of these T-shirts?

5. The price of a movie ticket for children under 12 is $6.75. How much would it cost for 8 ten-year-old children to go to the movies?

One-Digit by Three-Digit Multiplication

Class Activity

► Compare Multiplication Methods

Look at the drawing and the five numeric solutions for
237 × 4.

237 =	200	+	30	+	7
4	4 × 200 = 800		4 × 30 = 120	4 × 7=28	

Method A	Method B	Method C	Method D	Method E
237 = 200 + 30 + 7	237 = 200 + 30 + 7	237	237	$\overset{1\ 2}{237}$
× 4 = 4	× 4 = 4	× 4	× 4	× 4
4 × 200 = 800	800	800	28	948
4 × 30 = 120	120	120	120	
4 × 7 = 28	28	28	800	
948	948	948	948	

1. How are the solutions similar? List at least two ways.

2. How are the solutions different? List at least three
   comparisons between methods.

3. How do Methods A–D relate to the drawing? List at least
   two ways.

▶ **Analyze the Shortcut Method**

Look at this breakdown of solution steps for Method E.

Step 1	Step 2	Step 3
$\overset{2}{237}$	$\overset{12}{237}$	$\overset{12}{237}$
× 4	× 4	× 4
8	48	948

4. Describe what happens in Step 1.

5. Describe what happens in Step 2.

6. Describe what happens in Step 3.

Practice the Shortcut Method on these problems.

7. 349
    × 6

8. 768
    × 9

9. 632
    × 7

10 415
    × 3

▶ Round and Estimate With Hundreds and Tens

You can use what you know about rounding and multiplication with hundreds to estimate the product of 4 × 369.

11. Find the product if you round up: 4 × 400 = ▨

12. Find the product if you round down: 4 × 300 = ▨

13. Which one of the two estimates will be closer to the actual solution? Why?

14. Calculate the actual solution.

15. Explain why neither estimate is very close.

16. What would be the estimate if you added 50 × 4 to 300 × 4?

17. What would be the estimate if you added 70 × 4 to 300 × 4?

18. Estimate 4 × 782 by rounding 782 to the nearest hundred.

19. Find the actual product.

20. Find a better estimate for 4 × 782. Show your work.

Round, estimate, and fix the estimate as needed.

21. 6 × 309

22. 7 × 278

▶ One-Digit by Four-Digit Multiplication

You can use the multiplication methods you have learned to multiply a one-digit number by a four-digit number.

Find 8 × 3,248.

3,248 =	3,000	+	200	+	40	+	8	
8	8 × 3,000 = 24,000		8 × 200 = 1,600	8 × 40 = 320		8 × 8 = 64		8

Rectangle Sections Method

$$8 \times 3,000 = 24,000$$
$$8 \times 200 = 1,600$$
$$8 \times 40 = 320$$
$$8 \times 8 = 64$$
$$\overline{25,984}$$

Expanded Notation Method

$$3,248 = 3,000 + 200 + 40 + 8$$
$$\times \quad 8 = \qquad\qquad\qquad 8$$
$$8 \times 3,000 = 24,000$$
$$8 \times 200 = 1,600$$
$$8 \times 40 = 320$$
$$8 \times 8 = 64$$
$$\overline{25,984}$$

Algebraic Notation Method

$$8 \times 3,248 = 8 \times (3,000 + 200 + 40 + 8)$$
$$= (8 \times 3,000) + (8 \times 200) + (8 \times 40) + (8 \times 8)$$
$$= 24,000 \quad + 1,600 \quad + 320 \quad + 64$$
$$= 25,984$$

Make a rectangle drawing for each problem on your MathBoard. Then solve the problem using the method of your choice.

1. $3 \times 8,153 =$ ▨

2. $4 \times 2,961 =$ ▨

3. $6 \times 5,287 =$ ▨

4. $7 \times 1,733 =$ ▨

Practice One-Digit by Three-Digit Multiplication

▶ Too Much Information

A word problem may sometimes include more information than you need. Read the following problem and then answer each question.

Mrs. Sanchez is putting a border around her garden. Her garden is a rectangle with dimensions 12 feet by 18 feet. The border material costs $3.00 per foot. How many feet of border material is needed?

1. Identify any extra numerical information. Why isn't this information needed?

2. Solve the problem.

Solve each problem. Cross out information that is not needed.

Show your work on your paper or in your journal.

3. Judy bought a CD for $10. It has 13 songs. Each song is 3 minutes long. How long will it take to listen to the whole CD?

4. Jerry has 64 coins in his coin collection and 22 stamps in his stamp collection. His sister has 59 stamps in her collection. How many stamps do they have altogether?

5. Adrian has been playing the piano for 3 years. He practices 20 minutes a day. He is preparing for a recital that is 9 days away. How many minutes of practice will he do before the recital?

► Too Little Information

When solving problems in real life, you need to determine what information is needed to solve the problem. Read the following problem and then answer each question.

The campers and staff of a day camp are going to an amusement park on a bus. Each bus holds 26 people. How many buses will be needed?

6. Do you have enough information to solve this problem? What additional information do you need?

Determine if the problem can be solved. If it cannot be solved, tell what information is missing. If it can be solved, solve it.

7. Richard is saving $5 a week to buy a bike. When will he have enough money?

8. Natalie wants to find out how much her cat weighs. She picks him up and steps on the scale. Together they weigh 94 pounds. How much does the cat weigh?

9. Phyllis wants to make 8 potholders. She needs 36 loops for each potholder. How many loops does she need?

10. For one of the problems that could not be solved, rewrite it so it can be solved and solve it.

▶ Discuss Problems With Hidden Questions

Mrs. Norton bought 2 packages of white cheese with 8 slices in each pack. She bought 3 packages of yellow cheese with 16 slices in each pack. How many more slices of yellow cheese than white cheese did she buy?

1. What do you need to find?

2. What are the hidden questions?

3. Answer the hidden questions to solve the problem.

How many slices of white cheese? $2 \times 8 = $ ▮

How many slices of yellow cheese? $3 \times 16 = $ ▮

How many more slices of yellow cheese? $48 - 16 = $ ▮

Read the problem. Then answer the questions.

Maurice has 6 boxes of markers. June has 5 boxes. Each box contains 8 markers. How many markers do Maurice and June have altogether?

Show your work on your paper or in your journal.

4. Write the hidden questions.

5. Solve the problem.

▶ **Solve Problems With Hidden Questions**

Solve each problem and show your work.
Look for hidden questions. Label your answer.

Show your work on your paper or in your journal.

6. Mrs. Ortiz has 200 pink index cards. She has 3 packs of blue index cards with 75 cards in each pack. How many more blue index cards does she have?

7. Mr. Collins counts 54 cartons and 5 boxes of paper clips. Each carton contains 8 boxes. How many boxes of paper clips does he have?

8. Ms. Washington has 5 cartons of black printer ink. She has 4 cartons of color printer ink. Each carton contains 48 cartridges of ink. How many ink cartridges are there in all?

9. Mrs. Arnold has 6 reams of yellow paper. She also has 5 reams of blue paper. Each ream is 500 sheets of paper. How many sheets of paper does she have altogether?

10. Mr. Perez sells red, blue, pink, green, yellow, purple, silver, and gold gel pens. Each box contains 6 pens. There are 4 boxes of each color. How many gel pens does he have?

► Compare Models

The dot drawing, area model sketch, and Rectangle Sections
Method below all model the solution to 24 × 37.

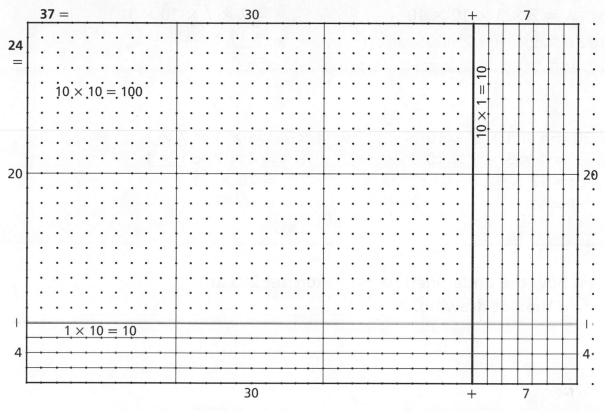

Area Model Sketch

Rectangle Sections Method

$$20 \times 30 = \mathbf{600}$$
$$20 \times 7 = \mathbf{140}$$
$$4 \times 30 = \mathbf{120}$$
$$\underline{4 \times 7 = \ \ \mathbf{28}}$$

1. Describe how each model shows 6 hundreds, 14 tens,
   12 tens, and 28 ones.

▶ **Investigate Products in the Sketch**

Complete each equation.

2. $20 \times 30 = 2 \times 10 \times 3 \times 10$
$= 2 \times 3 \times \underline{10 \times 10}$
$= 6 \times \blacksquare$
$= \blacksquare$

3. $20 \times 7 = 2 \times 10 \times 7 \times 1$
$= 2 \times 7 \times \underline{10 \times 1}$
$= 14 \times \blacksquare$
$= \blacksquare$

4. $4 \times 30 = 4 \times 1 \times 3 \times 10$
$= 4 \times 3 \times \underline{1 \times 10}$
$= 12 \times \blacksquare$
$= \blacksquare$

5. $4 \times 7 = 4 \times 1 \times 7 \times 1$
$= 4 \times 7 \times \underline{1 \times 1}$
$= 28 \times \blacksquare$
$= \blacksquare$

6. Explain how the underlined parts in exercises 2–5 are shown in the dot drawing.

7. Find 37×24 by adding the products in exercises 2–5.

▶ **Practice and Discuss Modeling**

Use your MathBoard to sketch an area drawing for each exercise. Then find the product.

8. 36×58

9. 28×42

10. 63×27

11. 26×57

12. 86×35

13. 38×65

► Compare Multiplication Methods

Study how these three methods of solving 43 × 67 are related to the area models.

Rectangle Sections Method

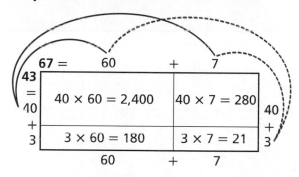

67 =	60	+	7	
43				
=				
40	40 × 60 = 2,400		40 × 7 = 280	40
+				+
3	3 × 60 = 180		3 × 7 = 21	3
	60	+	7	

$$40 \times 60 = 2{,}400$$
$$40 \times 7 = 280$$
$$3 \times 60 = 180$$
$$\underline{3 \times 7 = 21}$$
$$2{,}881$$

Expanded Notation Method

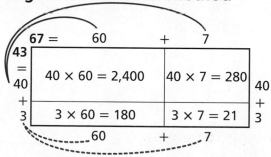

67 =	60	+	7	
43				
=				
40	40 × 60 = 2,400		40 × 7 = 280	40
+				+
3	3 × 60 = 180		3 × 7 = 21	3
	60	+	7	

$$67 \quad (60 + 7)$$
$$\underline{\times\ 43} = (40 + 3)$$
$$40 \times 60 = 2{,}400$$
$$40 \times 7 = 280$$
$$3 \times 60 = 180$$
$$\underline{3 \times 7 = 21}$$
$$2{,}881$$

Algebraic Notation Method

67 =	60	+	7	
43				
=				
40	40 × 60 = 2,400		40 × 7 = 280	40
+				+
3	3 × 60 = 180		3 × 7 = 21	3
	60	+	7	

$$43 \cdot 67 = (40 + 3) \cdot (60 + 7)$$
$$= 2{,}400 + 280 + 180 + 21$$
$$= 2{,}881$$

▶ The Shortcut Method

The steps for the Shortcut Method are shown below.

Step 1	Step 2	Step 3	Step 4	Step 5
$\overset{2}{6}7$	$\overset{2}{6}7$	$\overset{2}{\overset{2}{6}}7$	$\overset{2}{\overset{2}{6}}7$	$\overset{2}{\overset{2}{6}}7$
× 43	× 43	× 43	× 43	× 43
1	201	201	201	201
		8	268	+ 268
				2,881

Explain how the area drawing below relates to the Shortcut Method.

```
           67
      ┌──────────────────┐
   40 │  40 × 67 = 2,680  │
    + ├──────────────────┤
    3 │  3 × 67 = 201     │
      └──────────────────┘
```

Different Methods for Two-Digit Multiplication

Class Activity

▶ Estimate Products

Two-digit products can be **estimated** by **rounding** each number to the nearest ten.

Estimate and then solve.

1. 28 × 74

2. 84 × 27

3. 93 × 57

4. 87 × 54

5. 38 × 62

6. 65 × 39

7. 26 × 43

8. 59 × 96

9. 53 × 74

10. Write a multiplication word problem. Estimate the product and then solve.

11. Would using an estimate be problematic in the situation you wrote for exercise 10? Explain why or why not.

Going Further

▶ Multiplication and Money

You can estimate products involving money to help you plan a budget.

Estimate the amount needed and then find the exact cost.

Show your work on your paper or in your journal.

1. Kate wants to give her mother a bouquet of 38 helium balloons for her thirty-eighth birthday. The cost of an inflated helium balloon is $0.75. How much would it cost to inflate 38 of them?

2. When on vacation, John wants to buy a pencil souvenir for his 32 classmates. Each pencil costs $0.38. How much would 32 pencils cost?

3. Sally's family will be taking an 18-day vacation and needs to have someone take care of their cat while they are away. A veterinarian clinic charges $12 per day to care for a cat. How much would it cost them to have this clinic care for their cat for 18 days?

4. An airline charges each passenger $87.50 for a one-way airplane ticket. If the airplane holds 72 passengers, how much can the airline earn on that flight?

5. The entrance fee to an amusement park is $13.75. How much would it cost for 27 fourth-graders to go to the park?

Class Activity

▶ Practice Multiplication

With practice, you will be able to solve a multiplication problem using fewer written steps.

Solve.

> Show your work on your paper or in your journal.

1. Between his ninth and tenth birthdays, Jimmy read 1 book each week. If each book had about 95 pages, about how many pages did he read during the year?

2. Sam's father built a stone wall in their back yard. The wall was 14 stones high and 79 stones long. How many stones did he use to build the wall?

3. Balloon Bonanza sells 25 different kinds of balloons. They have 48 different colors of ribbon to tie onto the balloons. How many different combinations of balloons and ribbons does Balloon Bonanza sell?

4. Brian's Bike Shop sponsors a cross-country race every summer. Every rider gets an official race T-shirt. The first year of the race, 24 riders competed. Last year, 13 times as many riders competed. If T-shirts come in boxes of 100, how many boxes of T-shirts did Brian need to have for the race last year?

Going Further

▶ Lattice Multiplication

Discuss how each step of the "lattice" method shown below relates to the area drawing of 43 × 67. The lattice method was used hundreds of years ago. Sometimes people traced the lattice and wrote the numbers in the ground.

67 =	60	+	7	
43 = 40	40 × 60 = 2,400		40 × 7 = 280	40
+ 3	3 × 60 = 180		3 × 7 = 21	+ 3
	60	+	7	

Step 1

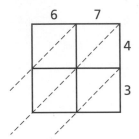

Step 2

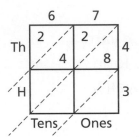

Step 3

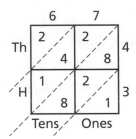

Step 4

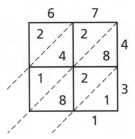

Step 5

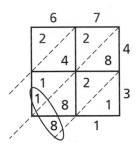

Step 6

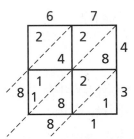

Step 7

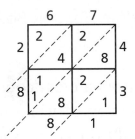

Step 8

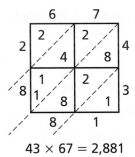

43 × 67 = 2,881

Copy each lattice. Use Lattice Multiplication to find each product.

1. 27 × 58 = ▇

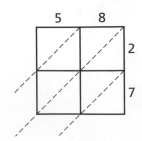

2. 65 × 87 = ▇

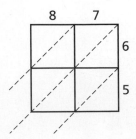

Practice Multiplication

5–15
Class Activity

▶ Use Rectangles to Multiply Hundreds

You can use a model to show multiplication with hundreds.
Study this model to see how we can multiply 300 × 7.

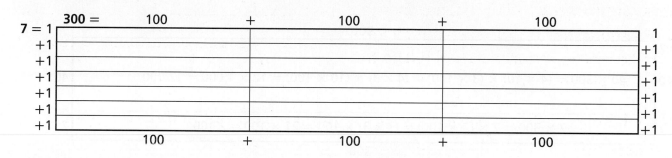

$$7 \times 300 = 7 \times (3 \times 100) = (7 \times 3) \times 100$$
$$= 21 \times 100$$
$$= 2,100$$

1. How many hundreds are represented in each column of the model?

2. How does knowing that 7 × 3 = 21 help you find 7 × 300?

3. What property of multiplication is used in the equation, 7 × (3 × 100) = (7 × 3) × 100?

4. Sketch a model of 400 × 6. Be ready to explain your model.

▶ Compare Three Methods

The Rectangle Sections, Expanded Notation, and Algebraic Method can be used to multiply numbers with hundreds.

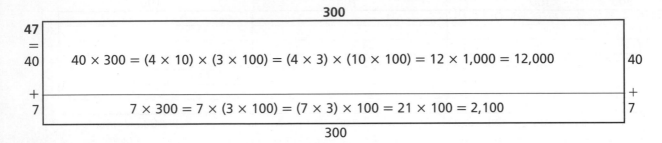

300

| 47 = 40 | $40 \times 300 = (4 \times 10) \times (3 \times 100) = (4 \times 3) \times (10 \times 100) = 12 \times 1{,}000 = 12{,}000$ | 40 |
| + 7 | $7 \times 300 = 7 \times (3 \times 100) = (7 \times 3) \times 100 = 21 \times 100 = 2{,}100$ | + 7 |

300

Rectangle Sections	**Expanded Notation**	**Algebraic Method**
12,000 + 2,100 ――――― 14,100	$47 = 40 + 7$ $\times\ \ 300 = \ \ \ \ 300$ ―――――――――― $300 \times 40 = 12{,}000$ $300 \times 7 = \ \ 2{,}100$ ――――――― $14{,}100$	$300 \cdot 47 = 300 \cdot (40 + 7)$ $= (300 \cdot 40) + (300 \cdot 7)$ $= 12{,}000 + 2{,}100$ $= 14{,}100$

5. Why does each solution above finish by adding 12,000 + 2,100?

6. How are the Expanded Notation and the Algebraic Method alike?

▶ Practice Multiplication With Hundreds

Multiply using your favorite method.

7. 9×600

8. 49×300

Multiplication With Hundreds

▶ Use Rectangles to Multiply Thousands

You can use a model to multiply very large numbers.
Notice that each of the smaller rectangles in this model
represents one thousand. Each of the columns represents
seven one-thousands or 7,000.

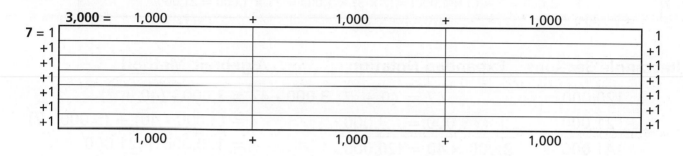

$$7 \times 3,000 = 7 \times (3 \times 1,000) = (7 \times 3) \times 1,000$$
$$= 21 \times 1,000$$
$$= 21,000$$

1. While multiplying by thousands, how many zeros can
   you expect in the product?

2. How does thinking of 3,000 as $3 \times 1,000$ help you to
   multiply $7 \times 3,000$?

3. Draw a model for $4 \times 8,000$. Then find the product.

▶ **Discuss and Compare Three Methods**

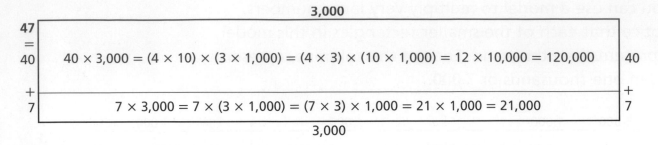

3,000

| 47 = 40 | $40 \times 3,000 = (4 \times 10) \times (3 \times 1,000) = (4 \times 3) \times (10 \times 1,000) = 12 \times 10,000 = 120,000$ | 40 |
| + 7 | $7 \times 3,000 = 7 \times (3 \times 1,000) = (7 \times 3) \times 1,000 = 21 \times 1,000 = 21,000$ | + 7 |

3,000

Rectangle Sections	**Expanded Notation**	**Algebraic Method**

Rectangle Sections:
$$120,000$$
$$+ \; 21,000$$
$$\overline{141,000}$$

Expanded Notation:
$$47 = 40 + 7$$
$$\times \; 3,000 = \quad 3,000$$
$$\overline{3,000 \times 40 = 120,000}$$
$$3,000 \times 7 = \quad 21,000$$
$$\overline{141,000}$$

Algebraic Method:
$$3,000 \cdot 47 = 3,000 \cdot (40 + 7)$$
$$= (3,000 \cdot 40) + (3,000 \cdot 7)$$
$$= 120,000 + 21,000$$
$$= 141,000$$

4. How is each step in the Expanded Notation Method represented in the rectangle model?

5. How are the Expanded Notation and Algebraic Method alike? How are they different?

Multiplication With Thousands

► Math and Social Studies

The timeline shows famous firsts in the history of airplane flight. The timeline is divided into 10-year periods called decades.

History of Airplane Flight

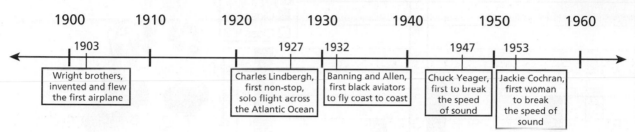

Solve.

1. Were the Lindbergh flight and the Banning and Allen flight in the same decade? Explain.

2. In 1947, Chuck Yaeger broke the speed of sound. About how many years before that did Lindbergh make his solo flight?

3. Before airplanes, people flew in hot-air balloons. On a separate piece of paper, make a timeline to show the events in the table shown.

Event	Year
First hot-air balloon flight	1783
First hot-air balloon flight by a women	1784
First hot-air balloon flight in the United States	1793

4. How many years elapsed between the first hot-air balloon flight and the first airplane flight?

5. Write an elapsed-time question that uses data from both timelines. Show the solution to the question.

▶ What's in the Salad?

A cafeteria has a salad bar. It includes lettuce and a choice of salad extras. The graph shows the results of a survey given to two fourth-grade classes about their favorite salad extra.

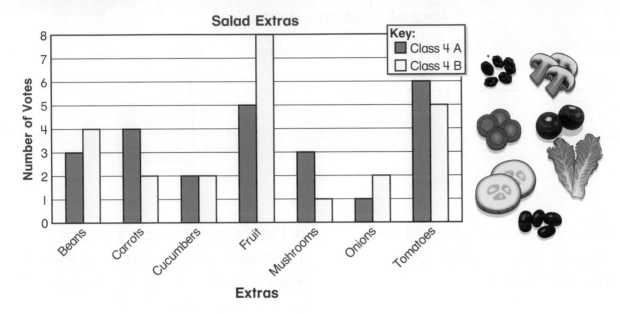

6. Which two extras appear to be the most popular? How do you know?

7. The cafeteria manager wants to limit the number of extras she needs to purchase. Which two would you recommend that she omit? Explain your reasoning.

8. If the cafeteria manager omits the two extras that you recommend, will every student's favorite extra be offered on some days? Explain your answer.

1. Use mental math to find each product.

4×7

4×70

40×70

Multiply, using any method. Show your work.

2. 68×3

3. 265×9

Estimate each product.

4. 33×66

5. 46×200

Solve, using any method. Show your work.

6. 52×47

7. 83×400

Solve each problem. List any extra numerical information.

Show your work on your paper or in your journal.

8. The fourth grade is collecting cans for a recycling center. There are 28 students in one class and 25 in another. Each student is asked to collect 15 cans. How many cans will these two classes collect in all?

9. A family spent 7 hours at the zoo. They bought 2 adult tickets for $20 each and 3 child tickets for $10 each. They bought lunch for $23. How much did the tickets cost?

10. **Extended Response** Sketch an area model for the product 23 × 6.

Explain how the area model you drew helps you to solve the multiplication problem 23 × 6.

► Parts of a Meter

Find these units on your meter strip.

Vocabulary

millimeter
centimeter
decimeter
meter

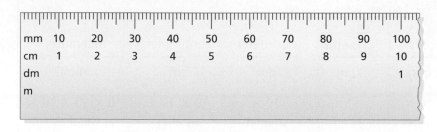

1. Find one **millimeter** (1 mm) on your strip.
   What objects are about 1 mm wide?

2. Find one **centimeter** (1 cm) on your strip.
   How many millimeters are in 1 cm?

3. What objects are about 1 cm wide?

4. Find one **decimeter** (1 dm) on your strip.
   How many centimeters are in 1 dm?

   This is one **meter** (1 m) that has been folded into
   decimeters to fit on the page.

5. How many decimeters are in 1 m?

Class Activity

► **Metric Prefixes**

Vocabulary

kilometer
prefixes
metric system

Units of Length

kilometer	hectometer	decameter	meter	decimeter	centimeter	millimeter
km	hm	dam	m	dm	cm	mm
10 × 10 × 10 × larger	10 × 10 × larger	10 × larger	1 m	10 × smaller	10 × 10 × smaller	10 × 10 × 10 × smaller
1 km = 1,000 m	1 hm = 100 m	1 dam = 10 m		10 dm = 1 m	100 cm = 1 m	1,000 mm = 1 m

6. What words do you know that can help you remember what the **prefixes** mean in the **metric system**?

7. How do the lengths of the different units relate to each other?

8. How many meters are in 1 **kilometer**?

9. How many millimeters are in 1 m?

10. How many centimeters are in 1 m?

11. What makes the metric system easy to understand?

▶ Choose Appropriate Units

Record which unit of length is best for measuring each object. Be prepared to justify your thinking in class.

12.

13.

14.

15.

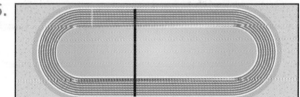

16.

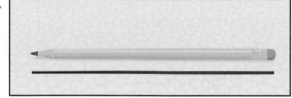

17.

18.

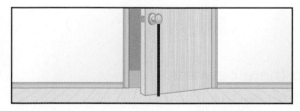

19.

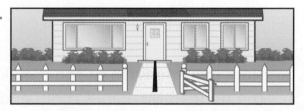

▶ Measure Distances

The fourth-grade classes at Lincoln School are exploring
metric measurements. This is a map of part of their school.

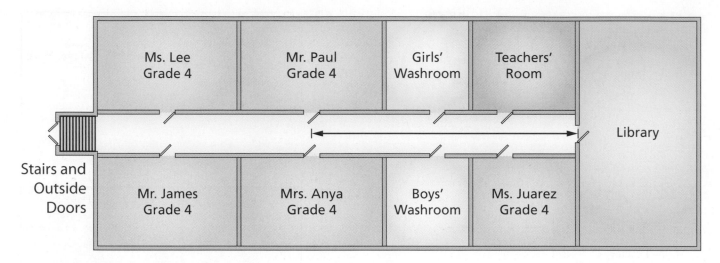

Key: ⊢—⊣ = 1 meter

Mr. Paul's students want to know the distance in whole
meters between the center of their classroom door and the
center of the door to the school library.

20. How can you use the map and the key to find the actual
    distance between two classroom doors?

21. How many lengths of the map key are there between
    the door to Mr. Paul's room and the door to the library?
    What is that distance in meters?

Your teacher will give you a copy of this letter.

Dear Family,

This mini-unit is about the metric measurement system. During this unit, students will become familiar with metric units of length or distance, capacity, mass, and temperature, as well as the size of each when compared to each other.

One **meter** is about the distance an adult man can reach, or a little longer than a yard.

One **liter** is about two large glasses of liquid, or a little more than a quart.

One **gram** is about the mass of a paper clip or a single peanut. One **kilogram** is a little more than 2 pounds.

Metric temperature is measured in **Celsius** degrees (°C). Water freezes at 0°C and boils at 100°C.

Students will also discover that the metric system is based on multiples of 10. Prefixes in the names of metric measurements tell the size of a measure compared to the size of the base unit.

Units of Length						
kilometer	hectometer	decameter	meter	decimeter	centimeter	millimeter
km	hm	dam	m	dm	cm	mm
10 × 10 × 10 × larger	10 × 10 × larger	10 × larger	1 m	10 × smaller	10 × 10 × smaller	10 × 10 × 10 × smaller
1 km = 1,000 m	1 hm = 100 m	1 dam = 10 m		10 dm = 1 m	100 cm = 1 m	1,000 mm = 1 m

The most commonly used length units are the **kilometer**, **meter**, **centimeter**, and **millimeter**.

The most commonly used capacity units are the **liter** and **milliliter**.

The most commonly used units of mass are the **gram**, **kilogram**, and **milligram**.

If you have any questions or comments, please call or write to me.

Sincerely,
Your child's teacher

Estimada familia:

Esta mini unidad trata del sistema métrico de medida. Los estudiantes se familiarizarán con unidades métricas de longitud o distancia, capacidad, masa y temperatura, así como con el tamaño de cada una comparada con las otras.

Un **metro** es aproximadamente la distancia que un hombre adulto puede alcanzar extendiendo el brazo, o un poco más de una yarda.

Un **litro** es aproximadamente dos vasos grandes de líquido, o un poco más de un cuarto de galón.

Un **gramo** es aproximadamente la masa de un sujetapapeles o un cacahuate. Un **kilogramo** es un poco más de 2 libras.

La temperatura métrica se mide en grados **Celsius** (°C). El agua se congela a 0°C y hierve a 100°C.

Los estudiantes también descubrirán que el sistema métrico está basado en múltiplos de 10. Los prefijos de los nombres de las medidas métricas indican el tamaño de la medida comparado con el tamaño de la unidad base.

Unidades de longitud						
kilómetro	hectómetro	decámetro	metro	decímetro	centímetro	milímetro
Km	Hm	Dm	m	dm	cm	mm
10 × 10 × 10 × más grande	10 × 10 × más grande	10 × más grande	1 m	10 × más pequeño	10 × 10 × más pequeño	10 × 10 × 10 × más pequeño
1 Km = 1,000 m	1 Hm = 100 m	1 Dm = 10 m		10 dm = 1 m	100 cm = 1 m	1,000 mm = 1 m

Las unidades de longitud más comunes son **kilómetro**, **metro**, **centímetro** y **milímetro**.

Las unidades de capacidad más comunes son **litro** y **mililitro**.

Las unidades de masa más comunes son **gramo**, **kilogramo** y **miligramo**.

Si tiene alguna pregunta o comentario, por favor comuníquese conmigo.

Atentamente,
El maestro de su niño

Class Activity

► Metric Units of Area

Vocabulary

square unit
square meter
square centimeter
square millimeter
square decimeter

Area is measured in **square units**, such as **square meters**.

This is one **square centimeter** (sq cm):

1. Why is it called a square unit?

This square centimeter is divided into **square millimeters** (sq mm):

2. How many sq mm are in 1 sq cm?

This array of square centimeters is one **square decimeter** (sq dm).

3. How many square centimeters are in 1 sq dm?

4. How many square millimeters are in 1 sq dm?

5. How many square decimeters are in 1 sq m? Explain.

6. How many square centimeters are in 1 sq m? How do you know?

▶ Measure Area

Ms. Juarez's students want to find the area of parts of their school.

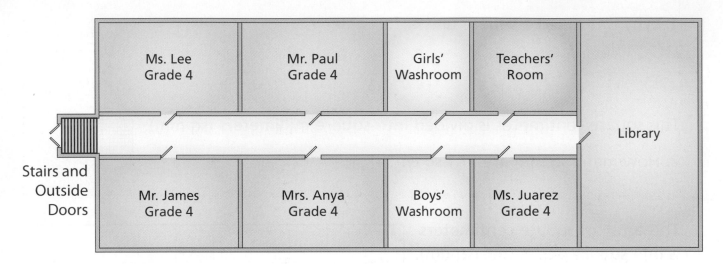

Key: ⊢⊣ = 1 meter

7. What measurements do Ms. Juarez's students need to find the area of the hallway between the stairs and the library door?

8. What do they need to do with their measurements to find the area?

9. What is the area of the library?

10. What is the area of the boys' and girls' washrooms combined?

Class Activity

► Convert Among Metric Units

Compare units of length or distance with units of area.

Units of Area						
square kilometer	hectare	are	square meter	square decimeter	square centimeter	square millimeter
sq km	ha	a	sq m	sq dm	sq cm	sq mm
100 × 100 × 100 × larger	100 × 100 × larger	100 × larger	1 sq m	100 × smaller	100 × 100 × smaller	100 × 100 × 100 × smaller
1 sq km = 1,000,000 sq m	1 ha = 10,000 sq m	1 a = 100 sq m		100 sq dm = 1 sq m	10,000 sq cm = 1 sq m	1,000,000 sq mm = 1 sq m

Solve.

11. How many meters long is each side of a square that has an area of 4 square meters (sq m)?

12. How many one-meter squares cover a square that has an area of 4 square meters (sq m)?

13. How many meters long is each side of a square that has an area of 4 **square kilometers** (sq km)?

14. How many one-meter squares cover a square that has an area of 4 sq km?

15. How is a square measurement unit like a square number in multiplication?

▶ Use a Simpler Problem

To solve a more difficult problem, sometimes you can think about a simpler problem.

1. Manuel cuts a length of rug into pieces of equal area. He cuts 8 square pieces like the one shown.

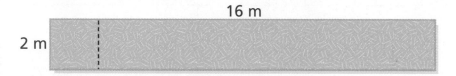

What is the area of each piece of rug?

Hint: What would the answer be if he made just one cut? two cuts?

2. Adita used square tiles to make a design. The sides of her tiles are 5 centimeters. She made a square design, using 36 of the tiles. What was the perimeter of her design?

Hint: What would the perimeter be if she used one-centimeter square tiles?

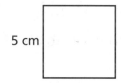

3. Adita used red and yellow tiles for her design in problem 2. She used one yellow tile for every three red tiles. How many of each color did she use?

4. **Challenge** How many different ways can you name a line segment, using any 2 of the first 8 letters of the alphabet?

Vocabulary
volume
cubic meter
cubic centimeter

▶ Visualize a Cubic Meter

The basic metric unit for measuring **volume** is a **cubic meter**.

This is a **cubic centimeter**.

Units of Volume			
cubic meter	**cubic decimeter**	**cubic centimeter**	**cubic millimeter**
cu m	cu dm	cu cm	cu mm
1 cu m	1,000 × smaller	1,000 × 1,000 × smaller	1,000 × 1,000 × 1,000 × smaller
	1,000 cu dm = 1 cu m	1,000,000 cu cm = 1 cu m	1,000,000,000 cu mm = 1 cu m

1. How many centimeters are equal to one meter?

2. How many cubic centimeters do you think you will need for a cubic meter?

3. What pattern do you see in the metric units of volume in the chart?

▶ Measure Volume

Each student at Lincoln School has a coat locker. Each locker is 1 meter high, 3 decimeters deep, and 5 decimeters across.

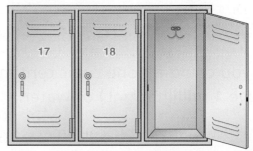

4. How can you find the total space inside a student locker?

5. What is the volume of each locker?

Class Activity

Vocabulary

Vocabulary

capacity
liter
milliliter
kiloliter

▶ Measure Capacity

The base metric unit of **capacity** is a **liter**.

Units of Capacity						
kiloliter	hectoliter	decaliter	liter	deciliter	centiliter	milliliter
kL	hL	daL	L	dL	cL	mL
10 × 10 × 10 × larger	10 × 10 × larger	10 × larger	1 L	10 × smaller	10 × 10 × smaller	10 × 10 × 10 × smaller
1 kL = 1,000 L	1 hL = 100 L	1 daL = 10 L		10 dL = 1 L	100 cL = 1 L	1,000 mL = 1 L

Ms. Lee's class cut a two-liter plastic bottle in half to make a one-liter jar. They marked the outside to show equal parts.

6. How many **milliliters** of water will fit in the jar?

7. How many of these jars will fill a **kiloliter** container? Explain why.

Here is a picture of a cubic centimeter.

If you could fill one cubic centimeter with water, you would have 1 milliliter (mL) of water.

8. How many cubic centimeters of water will Ms. Lee's jar hold? Explain why.

9. How many liters of water will fill a cubic decimeter?

Class Activity

► Measure Mass

Vocabulary

mass   tonne
gram   milligram
kilogram

The basic unit of **mass** is the **gram**.

Units of Mass						
kilogram	hectogram	decagram	gram	decigram	centigram	milligram
kg	hg	dag	g	dg	cg	mg
10 × 10 × 10 × larger	10 × 10 × larger	10 × larger	1 g	10 × smaller	10 × 10 × smaller	10 × 10 × 10 × smaller
1 kg = 1,000 g	1 hg = 100 g	1 dag = 10 g		10 dg = 1 g	100 cg = 1 g	1,000 mg = 1 g

1. How many **milligrams** are equal to 1 gram?

2. How many grams are equal to 1 kilogram?

Here is a picture of a cubic centimeter. You know that 1 cu cm can hold 1 mL of water. If you could weigh that amount of water, its mass would be one gram (1 g).

3. Is the gram a small or large unit of measurement? Explain your thinking.

Another common metric unit of mass is a **tonne**. It is equal to 1,000 **kilograms**.

4. How many grams are in a tonne?

5. Why is this very large unit of mass useful?

6. What might you measure in tonnes?

► Interpret a Bar Graph

Mrs. Anya's students graphed the masses of different dogs in the animal shelter.

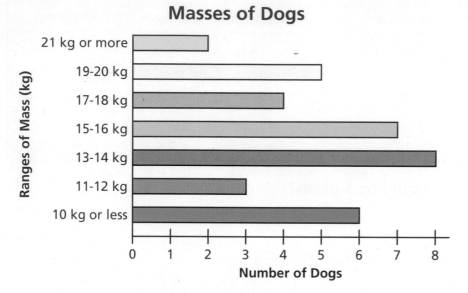

Masses of Dogs

7. How many dogs had a mass of 10 kilograms or less?

8. How many dogs had a mass of 21 kilograms or more?

9. Compare the number of dogs that had the greatest mass to the number of dogs that had the least mass. Describe the comparison as many ways as you can.

10. Write two different comparison statements about the dogs.

► Explore the Celsius Scale

The common temperature scale in the U.S. is called
Fahrenheit (°F). The metric temperature scale is called
Celsius (°C).

Equivalent Temperatures in Celsius and Fahrenheit

Temperature (°C)	⁻20	⁻10	0	10	20	30	40	50	60	70	80	90	100	110	120	130
Temperature (°F)	⁻4	14	32	50	68	86	104	122	140	158	176	194	212	230	248	266

1. What is the range of the Celsius temperatures on the table?

2. What is the range of the Fahrenheit temperatures on the table?

3. What happens to water at 32°F? What Celsius temperature is equivalent to 32°F?

4. What happens to water at 212°F? What Celsius temperature is equivalent to 212°F?

5. The temperature sign outside a bank reads 50°. Is this temperature a Celsius or a Fahrenheit reading? Explain.

6. If a Celsius thermometer shows 8°, what kind of clothing should you wear to be comfortable?

7. If puddles of water have a thin coating of ice on them, what is a reasonable estimate of the Celsius temperature?

8. A digital body thermometer says your body temperature is 39°C. Do you have a fever? How do you know?

▶ Write Equivalent Temperatures

Write an equivalent temperature. Use the chart on the previous page.

9. 40°F

10. 75°F

11. 0°F

12. 15°C

13. 35°C

14. ⁻15°C

▶ Relate Celsius Temperatures to Everyday Experiences

Each day of the school year, Mr. James's students measure the outside temperature in degrees Celsius (°C). They made a table of their results. This table shows four sample weeks from different times of the year.

Days	Week A					Week B					Week C					Week D				
	M	T	W	Th	F	M	T	W	Th	F	M	T	W	Th	F	M	T	W	Th	F
Temp. (°C)	⁻20	⁻19	⁻18	⁻4	⁻8	6	5	8	4	9	13	15	18	21	18	28	31	27	25	29

15. How is the temperature during Week A different from the temperature in Week D?

16. In your city, what month or months of the year could each week represent? Explain your thinking.

Write the best metric unit for each situation. Explain your thinking.

1. 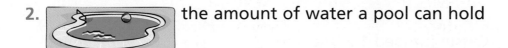 the length across a dime

2. the amount of water a pool can hold

3. the distance between two cities

4. the temperature of an oven

Write the correct metric unit to complete the equation.

5. 1 meter = 100

6. 1,000 millimeters = 1

7. 10 liters = 10,000

8. 1,000 grams = 1

Cassie entered the triple jump event at her school's field day. She made 3 attempts. Use this information to solve these word problems.

Show your work on your paper or in your journal.

9. In her first attempt, Cassie jumped 1,210 cm in total. In her second attempt, she jumped 1,180 cm in total. How much farther, in centimeters, did she jump on the better of the two attempts?

10. **Extended Response** In her third attempt, Cassie jumped 48 dm, 340 cm, and 4 m. What is the total distance, in centimeters, that Cassie jumped? Explain your answer.

Glossary

A

acre A measure of land area. An acre is equal to 4,840 square yards.

acute angle An angle smaller than a right angle.

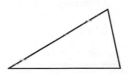

acute triangle A triangle with three acute angles.

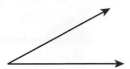

addend One of two or more numbers added together to find a sum.

Example:

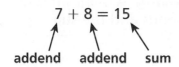
$$7 + 8 = 15$$

addend   addend   sum

analog clock A clock with a face and hands.

angle A figure formed by two rays with the same endpoint.

array An arrangement of objects, symbols, or numbers in rows and columns.

area The amount of surface covered or enclosed by a figure measured in square units.

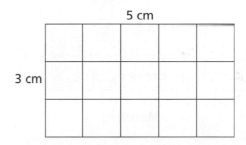

Associative Property of Addition Grouping the addends in different ways does not change the sum.

Example: $3 + (5 + 7) = 15$
$(3 + 5) + 7 = 15$

Associative Property of Multiplication Grouping the factors in different ways does not change the product.

Example: $3 \times (5 \times 7) = 105$
$(3 \times 5) \times 7 = 105$

Glossary (Continued)

average (mean) The size of each of *n* equal groups made from *n* data values. It is calculated by adding the values and dividing by *n*.

Example: 75, 84, 89, 91, 101
$75 + 84 + 89 + 91 + 101 = 440,$
then $440 \div 5 = 88$. The average is 88.

B

bar graph A graph that uses bars to show data. The bars may be vertical or horizontal.

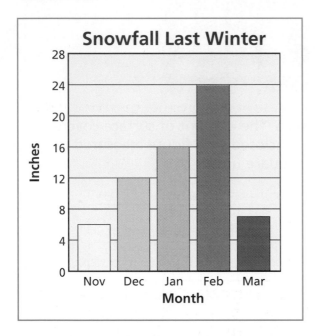

base For a triangle or parallelogram, a base is any side. For a trapezoid, a base is either of the parallel sides. For a prism, a base is one of the congruent parallel faces that may not be rectangular. For a pyramid, the base is the face that does not touch the vertex of the pyramid.

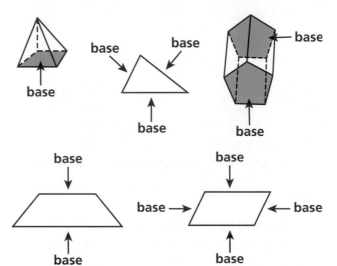

break-apart drawing A diagram that shows two addends and the sum.

C

capacity A measure of how much a container can hold.

Celsius The metric temperature scale.

center The point that is the same
distance from every point on the circle.

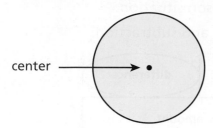

center

centimeter A unit of measure in the
metric system that equals one
hundredth of a meter. 1 cm = 0.01 m

change minus A change situation that
can be represented by subtraction. In a
change minus situation, the starting
number, the change, or the result will
be unknown.

Example:

Unknown Start	Unknown Change	Unknown Result
$n - 2 = 3$	$5 - n = 3$	$5 - 2 = n$

change plus A change situation that can
be represented by addition. In a change
plus situation, the starting number, the
change, or the result will be unknown.

Example:

Unknown Start	Unknown Change	Unknown Result
$n + 2 = 5$	$3 + n = 5$	$3 + 2 = n$

circle A plane figure that forms a closed
path so that all the points on the path
are the same distance from a point
called the center.

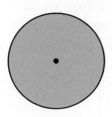

circle graph A graph that uses parts of a
circle to show data.

Example:

Favorite Fiction Books

circumference The distance around a
circle.

closed Having no endpoints.

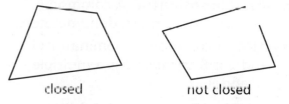

closed   not closed

collection situations Situations that
involve putting together (joining) or
taking apart (separating) groups.

column A part of a table or array that
contains items arranged vertically.

• • • •
• • • •
• • • •
• • • •

Glossary (Continued)

combination situation A situation in which the number of possible different combinations is determined. A table can sometimes be used to show all possible combinations; multiplication can be used to calculate the number of combinations.

Example:

Different Sandwich Combinations

	peanut butter	cheese	turkey
wheat bread	peanut butter on wheat bread	cheese on wheat bread	turkey on wheat bread
white bread	peanut butter on white bread	cheese on white bread	turkey on white bread

Number of combinations = 3 × 2 = 6

common denominator A common multiple of two or more denominators.

Example: A common denominator of $\frac{1}{2}$ and $\frac{1}{3}$ is 6 because 6 is a multiple of 2 and 3.

Commutative Property of Addition Changing the order of addends does not change the sum.

Example: 3 + 8 = 11
8 + 3 = 11

Commutative Property of Multiplication Changing the order of factors does not change the product.

Example: 3 × 8 = 24
8 × 3 = 24

comparison bars Bars that represent the larger amount and smaller amount in a comparison situation.

For addition and subtraction:

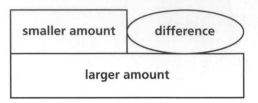

For multiplication and division:

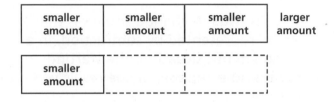

comparison situation A situation in which two amounts are compared by addition or by multiplication. An *additive comparison situation* compares by asking or telling how much more (how much less) one amount is than another. A *multiplicative comparison situation* compares by asking or telling how many times as many one amount is as another. The multiplicative comparison may also be made using fraction language. For example, you can say, "Sally has one fourth as much as Tom has," instead of saying "Tom has 4 times as much as Sally has."

complex figure A figure made by combining simple geometric figures like rectangles and triangles. The factor pairs of 18 are 1 and 18, 2 and 9, 3 and 6.

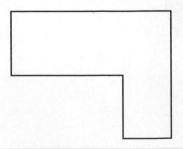

composite number A number greater than 1 that has more than one factor pair. Examples of composite numbers are 10 and 18. The factor pairs of 10 are 1 and 10, 2 and 5. The factor pairs of 18 are 1 and 18, 2 and 9, 3 and 6.

concave A polygon is concave if at least one diagonal is outside of the polygon.

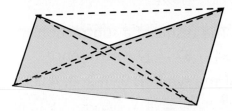

cone A solid figure with a curved base and a single vertex.

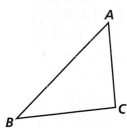

circular cone

congruent Exactly the same size and shape.

Example: Triangles *ABC* and *PQR* are congruent.

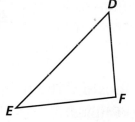

convex A polygon is convex if all of the diagonals are inside the polygon.

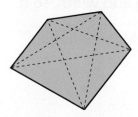

cube A solid figure that has 6 faces that are congruent squares.

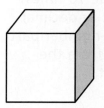

cubic centimeter A metric unit for measuring volume. It is the volume of a cube with one-centimeter edges.

cubic foot A unit for measuring volume. It is the volume of a cube with one-foot edges.

cubic inch A unit for measuring volume. It is the volume of a cube with one-inch edges.

cubic meter A metric unit for measuring volume. It is the volume of a cube with one-meter edges.

cubic yard A unit for measuring volume. It is the volume of a cube with one-yard edges.

cylinder A solid figure with two congruent curved bases.

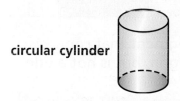

circular cylinder

D

data A collection of information.

Glossary (Continued)

decimal number A representation of a number using the numerals 0 to 9, in which each digit has a value 10 times the digit to its right. A dot or **decimal point** separates the whole-number part of the number on the left from the fractional part on the right.

Examples: 1.23 and 0.3

decimal point A symbol used to separate dollars and cents in money amounts or to separate ones and tenths in decimal numbers.

Examples:

$8.59   1.2

decimal point

decimeter A unit of measure in the metric system that equals one tenth of a meter. 1 dm = 0.1 m

denominator The number below the bar in a fraction. It shows the total number of equal parts in the fraction.

Example:

$\frac{3}{4}$ ◄— denominator

diagonal A line segment that connects vertices of a polygon, but is not a side of the polygon.

diagonal

diameter A line segment from one side of a circle to the other through the center. Also the length of that segment.

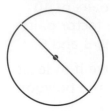

difference The result of a subtraction.

Example: 54 − 37 = 17 ◄ difference

digit Any of the symbols 0, 1, 2, 3, 4, 5, 6, 7, 8, or 9.

digital clock A clock that shows us the hour and minutes with numbers.

Digit-by-Digit A method used to solve a division problem.

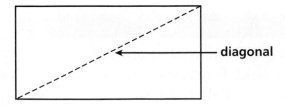

Put in only one digit at a time.

```
        5                54               546
  7) 3,822          7) 3,822         7) 3,822
   − 3 5             − 3 5            − 3 5
     32                32               32
                     − 28             − 28
                       42               42
                                      − 42
```

dimension The height, length, or width.

Examples:

A line segment has only length, so it has *one* dimension.

A rectangle has length and width, so it has *two* dimensions.

A cube has length, width, and height, so it has *three* dimensions.

Distributive Property You can multiply a sum by a number, or multiply each addend by the number and add the products; the result is the same.

Example:
$$3 \times (2 + 4) = (3 \times 2) + (3 \times 4)$$
$$3 \times 6 \quad = \quad 6 \quad + \quad 12$$
$$18 \quad = \quad \quad 18$$

dividend The number that is divided in division.
Example: $9\overline{)63}$, 63 is the dividend.

divisor The number you divide by in division.
Example: $9\overline{)63}$, 9 is the divisor.

dot array An arrangement of dots in rows and columns.

double bar graph Data is compared by using pairs of bars drawn next to each other.

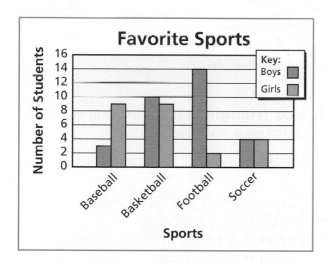

edge The line segment where two faces of a three-dimensional figure meet.

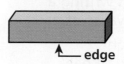
edge

equally likely In probability, equally likely means having the same chance of occurring.

Example: When flipping a coin, the coin is **equally likely** to land on heads or tails.

Equal-Shares Drawing A diagram that shows a number separated into equal parts.

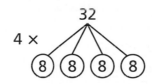

equation A statement that two expressions are equal. It has an equals sign.

Examples: $32 + 35 = 67$
$67 = 32 + 34 + 1$
$(7 \times 8) + 1 = 57$

equilateral Having all equal sides.

Example: An equilateral triangle

equivalent fractions Two or more fractions that represent the same number.

Example: $\frac{2}{4}$ and $\frac{4}{8}$ are equivalent because they both represent one half.

Glossary (Continued)

estimate A number close to an exact amount or to find about how many or how much.

expanded form A way of writing a number that shows the value of each of its digits.

Example: Expanded form of 835:
800 + 30 + 5
8 hundreds + 3 tens + 5 ones

Expanded Notation A method used to solve multiplication and division problems.

Examples:

$$43 \times 67$$

$$
\begin{array}{r}
67 = 60 + 7 \\
\times\, 43 = 40 + 3 \\
\hline
40 \times 60 = 2400 \\
40 \times 7 = 280 \\
3 \times 60 = 180 \\
3 \times 7 = +21 \\
\hline
2{,}881
\end{array}
$$

$$3{,}822 \div 7$$

$$
\begin{array}{r}
6 \\
40 \\
500
\end{array}\Big) 546
$$

$$
\begin{array}{r}
7\,)\,3{,}822 \\
-\,3\,500 \\
\hline
322 \\
-\,280 \\
\hline
42 \\
-\,42 \\
\hline
0
\end{array}
$$

expression One or more numbers, variables, or numbers and variables with one or more operations.

Examples: 4
6x
6x − 5
7 + 4

face A flat surface of a three-dimensional figure.

factor One of two or more numbers multiplied to find a product.

Example:

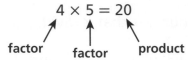

$$4 \times 5 = 20$$

factor   factor   product

Factor Fireworks Shows how a whole number can be broken down into a product of prime factors.

12

This is also called a **Factor Tree.**

2   ×   6

3 × 2

factor pair A factor pair for a number is a pair of whole numbers whose product is that number.

Example:

$$5 \times 7 = 35$$

factor   product
pair

Factor Triangle A diagram that shows a factor pair and the product.

Example:

32

÷ /\ ÷

4 × 8

Fahrenheit The temperature scale used in the United States.

Fast Array A numerical form of an array that shows an unknown factor or unknown product.

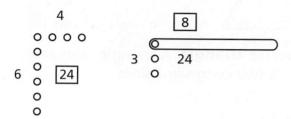

foot A U.S. customary unit of length equal to 12 inches.

fraction A number that is the sum of unit fractions, each an equal part of a set or part of a whole.

Examples: $\frac{3}{4} = \frac{1}{4} + \frac{1}{4} + \frac{1}{4}$

$\frac{5}{4} = \frac{1}{4} + \frac{1}{4} + \frac{1}{4} + \frac{1}{4} + \frac{1}{4}$

frequency table A table that shows how many times each event, item, or category occurs.

Frequency Table	
Height	Frequency
47	1
48	2
49	4
50	3
51	1
52	0
53	2
Total	13

function A set of ordered pairs of numbers such that for every first number there is only one possible second number.

Example: The relationship between yards and feet.

Yards	1	2	3	4	5	6	7
Feet	3	6	9	12	15	18	21

function table A table of ordered pairs that shows a function.

Rule: add 2		Heads	1	2	3	4
Input	Output	Legs	2	4	6	8
1	3					
2	4					
3	5					
4	6					

G

gram The basic unit of mass in the metric system.

greater than (>) A symbol used to compare two numbers. The greater number is given first below.

Example: 33 > 17
33 is greater than 17.

greatest Largest. Used to order three or more quantities or numbers.

H

height The perpendicular distance from a base of a figure to the highest point.

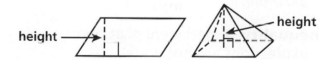

horizontal bar graph A bar graph with horizontal bars.

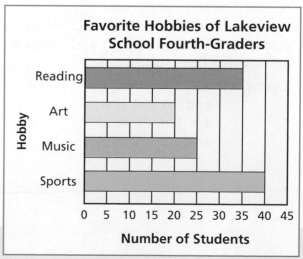

Glossary (Continued)

hundredth A unit fraction representing one of one hundred parts, written as 0.01 or $\frac{1}{100}$.

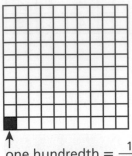

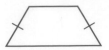

one hundredth $= \frac{1}{100} = 0.01$

I

Identity Property of Multiplication The product of 1 and any number equals that number.

Example: $10 \times 1 = 10$

improper fraction A fraction that is greater than or equal to 1. The numerator is greater than or equal to the denominator.

Examples: $\frac{13}{4}$ or $\frac{4}{4}$

inch A U.S. customary unit of length.

Example:

1 inch

inequality A statement that two expressions are not equal.

Examples: $2 < 5$
$4 + 5 > 12 - 8$

inverse operations Opposite or reverse operations that undo each other. Addition and subtraction are inverse operations. Multiplication and division are inverse operations.

Examples: $4 + 6 = 10$ so, $10 - 6 = 4$
and $10 - 4 = 6$.
$3 \times 9 = 27$ so, $27 \div 9 = 3$
and $27 \div 3 = 9$.

isosceles trapezoid A trapezoid with a pair of opposite congruent sides.

isosceles triangle A triangle with at least two congruent sides.

K

kilogram A unit of mass in the metric system that equals one thousand grams. 1 kg = 1,000 g

kiloliter A unit of capacity in the metric system that equals one thousand liters. 1 kL = 1,000 L

L

least Smallest. Used to order three or more quantities or numbers.

least common denominator The least common multiple of two or more denominators.

Example: The least common denominator of $\frac{1}{2}$ and $\frac{1}{3}$ is 6 because 6 is the smallest multiple of 2 and 3.

length The measure of a line segment or one side or edge of a figure.

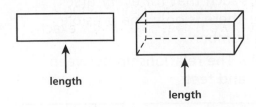

length   length

less than (<) A symbol used to compare two numbers. The smaller number is given first below.

Example: 54 < 78
54 is less than 78.

line A straight path that goes on forever in opposite directions.

Example: line *AB*

line of symmetry A line that divides a figure into two congruent parts.

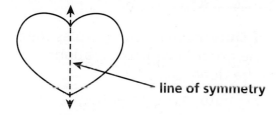

line plot A diagram that shows the frequency of data on a number line.

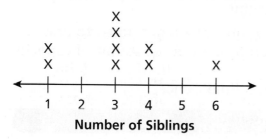

Number of Siblings

line segment Part of a line that has two endpoints.

line symmetry A figure has line symmetry if it can be folded along a line to create two halves that match exactly.

liter The basic unit of capacity in the metric system. 1 liter = 1,000 milliliters.

M

mass The measure of the amount of matter in an object.

mean (average) The size of each of *n* equal groups made from *n* data values. It is calculated by adding the values and dividing by *n*.

Examples: 75, 84, 89, 91, 101
75 + 84 + 89 + 91 + 101 = 440,
then 440 ÷ 5 = 88. The mean is 88.

measure of central tendency The mean, median, or mode of a set of numbers.

median The middle number in a set of ordered numbers. For an even number of numbers, the median is the average of the two middle numbers.

Examples: 13   26   34   47   52
The median for this set is 34.

8   8   12   14   20   21
The median for this set is
(12 + 14) ÷ 2 = 13.

meter The basic unit of length in the metric system.

mile A U.S. customary unit of length equal to 5,280 feet.

milligram A unit of mass in the metric system that equals one thousandth of a gram. 1 mg = 0.001 g

milliliter A unit of capacity in the metric system that equals one thousandth of a liter. 1 mL = 0.001 L

millimeter A unit of length in the metric system that equals one thousandth of a meter. 1 mm = 0.001 m

Glossary (Continued)

misleading language Language in a comparing sentence that may cause you to do the wrong operation.

> Example: John's age is 3 *more than* Jessica's. If John is 12, how old is Jessica?

mixed number A number that can be represented by a whole number and a fraction.

> Example: $4\frac{1}{2} = 4 + \frac{1}{2}$

mode The number that appears most frequently in a set of numbers.

> Example: 2, 4, 4, 4, 5, 7, 7
> 4 is the mode in this set of numbers.

N

net A flat pattern that can be folded to make a solid figure.

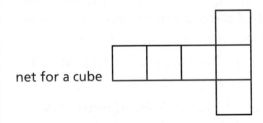

net for a cube

number sentence A mathematical statement that uses =, <, or > to show how numbers or expressions are related. The types of number sentences are equations and inequalities.

> Example: 25 + 25 = 50
> 13 > 8 + 2

numerator The number above the bar in a fraction. It shows the number of equal parts.

> Example:

$\frac{3}{4}$ ⟵ numerator $\frac{3}{4} = \frac{1}{4} + \frac{1}{4} + \frac{1}{4}$

O

obtuse angle An angle greater than a right angle and less than a straight angle.

obtuse triangle A triangle with one obtuse angle.

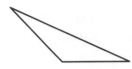

Order of Operations A set of rules that state the order in which operations should be done.

> STEPS: -Compute inside parentheses first.
> -Multiply and divide from left to right.
> -Add and subtract from left to right.

ounce A unit of weight equal to one sixteenth of a pound. A unit of capacity equal to one eighth of a cup (also called a fluid ounce).

P

parallel Lines in the same plane that never intersect are parallel. Line segments and rays that are part of parallel lines are also parallel.

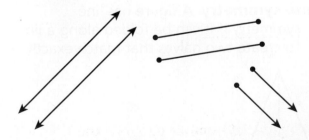

parallelogram A quadrilateral with both pairs of opposite sides parallel.

Partial-Quotients Method A method used to solve division problems where the partial quotients are written next to the division problem instead of above it.

Example:

$$\begin{array}{r|r} 8)\overline{178} & \\ -\ 160 & 20 \\ \hline 18 & \\ -\ 16 & 2 \\ \hline 2 & 22 \\ \end{array}$$

22 R2

pentagon A polygon with five sides.

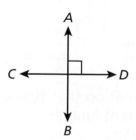

perimeter The distance around a figure.

perpendicular Lines, line segments, or rays are perpendicular if they form right angles.

Example: These two line segments are perpendicular.

pi A special number equal to the circumference of a circle divided by its diameter. Pi can be represented by the symbol π and is approximately 3.14.

pictograph A graph that uses pictures or symbols to represent data.

Books Checked Out of Library	
Student	
Najee	📖 📖
Tariq	📖 📖 📖 📖 📖 📖
Celine	📖 📖 📖 📖 📖 📖 📖 📖
Jamarcus	📖 📖 📖
Brooke	📖 📖 📖 📖

📖 = 5 books

place value The value assigned to the place that a digit occupies in a number.

Example: 235
          ↑

The 2 is in the hundreds place, so its value is 200.

plane A flat surface that extends without end.

polygon A closed plane figure with sides made of straight line segments.

pound A unit of weight in the U.S. customary system.

prime number A number greater than 1 that has 1 and itself as the only factor pair. Examples of prime numbers are 2, 7, and 13. The only factor pair of 7 is 1 and 7.

prism A solid figure with two congruent parallel bases joined by rectangular faces. Prisms are named by the shape of their bases.

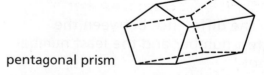

pentagonal prism

probability A number between 0 and 1 that represents the chance of an event happening.

Glossary (Continued)

product The answer to a multiplication.

Example: $9 \times 7 = 63$

product

pyramid A solid with a polygon for a base whose faces meet at a point called the vertex.

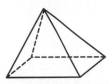

Q

quadrilateral A polygon with four sides.

quotient The answer to a division problem.

Example: $9\overline{)63}$; 7 is the quotient.

R

radius A line segment that connects the center of a circle to any point on that circle. Also the length of that line segment.

range The difference between the greatest number and the least number in a set.

ray Part of a line that has one endpoint and extends without end in one direction.

rectangle A parallelogram with four right angles.

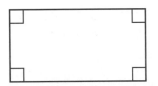

Rectangle Sections A method using rectangle drawings to solve multiplication or division problems.

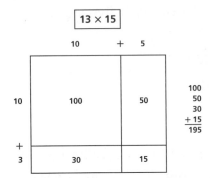

reflection A transformation that flips a figure onto a congruent image. Sometimes called a *flip*.

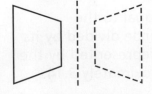

regular polygon Having all sides and angles congruent.

Example: A square is a regular quadrilateral.

remainder The number left over after dividing two numbers that are not evenly divisible.

Example: 5)43 8 R3   The remainder is 3.

Repeated Groups situation A multiplication situation in which all groups have the same number of objects.

rhombus A parallelogram with congruent sides.

right angle One of four congruent angles made by perpendicular lines.

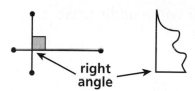

right angle

right triangle A triangle with one right angle.

round To find the nearest ten, hundred, thousand, or some other place value. The usual rounding rule is to round up if the next digit to the right is 5 or more and round down if the next digit to the right is less than 5.

Examples: 463 rounded to the nearest ten is 460.

463 rounded to the nearest hundred is 500.

row A part of a table or array that contains items arranged horizontally.

S

scalene A triangle with no equal sides is a scalene triangle.

simplest form A fraction is in simplest form if there is no whole number (other than 1) that divides evenly into the numerator and denominator.

Examples: $\frac{3}{4}$ This fraction is in simplest form because no number divides evenly into 3 and 4.

Glossary (Continued)

simplify a fraction To divide the numerator and the denominator of a fraction by the same number to make an equivalent fraction made from fewer but larger unit fractions.

Example: $\frac{5}{10} = \frac{5 \div 5}{10 \div 5} = \frac{1}{2}$

situation equation An equation that shows the action or the relationship in a problem.

Example: $35 + n = 40$

slant height The height of a triangular face of a pyramid.

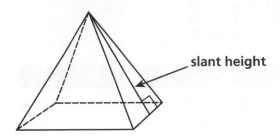
slant height

solution equation An equation that shows the operation to perform in order to solve the problem.

Examples: $n = 40 - 35$

sphere A solid figure shaped like a ball.

square array An array in which the number of rows equals the number of columns.

square centimeter A unit of area equal to the area of a square with one-centimeter sides.

square decimeter A unit of area equal to the area of a square with one-decimeter sides.

square foot A unit of area equal to the area of a square with one-foot sides.

square inch A unit of area equal to the area of a square with one-inch sides.

square kilometer A unit of area equal to the area of a square with one-kilometer sides.

square meter A unit of area equal to the area of a square with one-meter sides.

square mile A unit of area equal to the area of a square with one-mile sides.

square millimeter A unit of area equal to the area of a square with one-millimeter sides.

square number The product of a whole number and itself.

Example: $3 \times 3 = 9$
9 is a square number.

square unit A unit of area equal to the area of a square with one-unit sides.

square yard A unit of area equal to the area of a square with one-yard sides.

standard form The form of a number written using digits.

Example: 2,145

sum The answer when adding two or more addends.

Example:

$$53 + 26 = 79$$

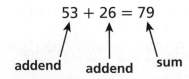
addend   addend   sum

surface area The total area of the two-dimensional surfaces of a three-dimensional figure.

T

table Data arranged in rows and columns.

tally chart A chart that uses tally marks to record and organize data.

Tally Chart	
Height (inches)	Tally
47	///
48	ⵀⵀ
49	//
50	
51	ⵀⵀ /
52	////
53	//

/ is 1

ⵀⵀ is 5

tenth A unit fraction representing one of ten equal parts of a whole, written as 0.1 or $\frac{1}{10}$.

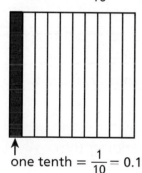

12.34
↑
tenth

one tenth $= \frac{1}{10} = 0.1$

thousandth A unit fraction representing one of one thousand equal parts of a whole, written as 0.001 or $\frac{1}{1,000}$.

ton A unit of weight that equals 2,000 pounds.

total Sum. The result of addition.

Example:

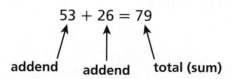

53 + 26 = 79

addend   addend   total (sum)

translation A transformation that moves a figure along a straight line without turning or flipping. Sometimes called a *slide*.

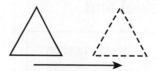

trapezoid A quadrilateral with one pair of parallel sides.

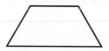

triangle A polygon with three sides.

U

unit A standard of measurement.

Examples: Centimeters, pounds, inches, and so on.

unit fraction A fraction whose numerator is 1. It shows one equal part of a whole.

Example: $\frac{1}{4}$

V

vertex A point that is shared by two sides of an angle, two sides of a polygon, or edges of a solid figure.

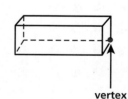

vertex   vertex   vertex

Glossary (Continued)

vertical bar graph A bar graph with vertical bars.

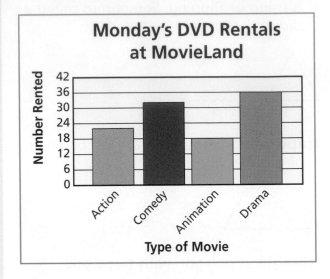

volume The number of cubic units of space occupied by a solid figure.

 W

width The measure of one side or edge of a figure.

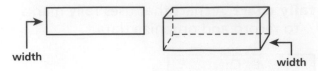

word form The form of a number written using words instead of digits.

Example: Six hundred thirty-nine

 **Y**

yard A U.S. customary unit of length equal to 3 feet.

A

×	1	2	3	4	5	6	7	8	9	10
1	1	2	3	4	5	6	7	8	9	10
2	2	4	6	8	10	12	14	16	18	20
3	3	6	9	12	15	18	21	24	27	30
4	4	8	12	16	20	24	28	32	36	40
5	5	10	15	20	25	30	35	40	45	50
6	6	12	18	24	30	36	42	48	54	60
7	7	14	21	28	35	42	49	56	63	70
8	8	16	24	32	40	48	56	64	72	80
9	9	18	27	36	45	54	63	72	81	90
10	10	20	30	40	50	60	70	80	90	100

B

×	3	5	1	4	2	8	9	7	10	6
3	9	15	3	12	6	24	27	21	30	18
5	15	25	5	20	10	40	45	35	50	30
1	3	5	1	4	2	8	9	7	10	6
4	12	20	4	16	8	32	36	28	40	24
2	6	10	2	8	4	16	18	14	20	12
8	24	40	8	32	16	64	72	56	80	48
9	27	45	9	36	18	72	81	63	90	54
7	21	35	7	28	14	56	63	49	70	42
10	30	50	10	40	20	80	90	70	100	60
6	18	30	6	24	12	48	54	42	60	36

C

×	2	3	5	4	9	5	9	2	4	3
2	4	6	10	8	18	10	18	4	8	6
3	6	9	15	12	27	15	27	6	12	9
5	10	15	25	20	45	25	45	10	20	15
4	8	12	20	16	36	20	36	8	16	12
9	18	27	45	36	81	45	81	18	36	27
6	12	18	30	24	54	30	54	12	24	18
7	14	21	35	28	63	35	63	14	28	21
8	16	24	40	32	72	40	72	16	32	24
6	12	18	30	24	54	30	54	12	24	18
8	16	24	40	32	72	40	72	16	32	24

D

×	6	7	8	7	8	6	8	7	6	8
1	6	7	8	7	8	6	8	7	6	8
2	12	14	16	14	16	12	16	14	12	16
5	30	35	40	35	40	30	40	35	30	40
10	60	70	80	70	80	60	80	70	60	80
3	18	21	24	21	24	18	24	21	18	24
4	24	28	32	28	32	24	32	28	24	32
6	36	42	48	42	48	36	48	42	36	48
7	42	49	56	49	56	42	56	49	42	56
8	48	56	64	56	64	48	64	56	48	64
9	54	63	72	63	72	54	72	63	54	72